Myths, Gods, Machines

Myths, Gods, Machines

Illuminations on

Mythology, History

and Science

John David Ebert

ISBN: 978-0-9971356-1-9

Post Egoism Media | Eugene, Oregon

This book is dedicated to Julian Samuel Ebert.

Cover design by
J.D. Casten

Contents

Preface

The essays collected in this book constitute, as it were, a sort of retrospective of two decades as an American cultural critic. None have previously appeared in book form, however, and most of them have never been published before. Only the first two essays, "Visions of a Biomechanical Apocalypse (First Version)" and "Ancient Myth and Modern Science" were published in periodicals (the now defunct *Lapis* and *Parabola* magazine, respectively).[1] I did "publish" my essay about the Unabomber on my blog at cultural-discourse.com, and also my piece on Thomas Pynchon's novel *V.* that concludes this collection, but those essays are no longer available on my web site. The rest of the essays were simply lying around on my laptop in varying stages of completion, and all have been rewritten, polished, and given new coats of paint.

The essays were selected by me for this collection because they all hover around what has been the core theme of my career as a cultural critic: namely, the tensions between ancient ritual, symbol and myth on the one hand, and the constant barrage of technological innovations on the other, innovations that have destabilized these traditions, sometimes wiping them out completely, and at other times discrediting the transcendental spinal axes holding them upright. Gianni Vattimo has not called this the age of "soft truths" for nothing.[2]

As any reader of my books knows very well, I never arrange my essays haphazardly, and the case is no less so with the present collection despite its apparent diversity, for it is arranged in "epochs" in order to tell a story: the history of the transformation of the gods into consumer icons and pop culture signifiers. The opening two essays in the section entitled "Tensions Between Myth and Science" form a sort of prologue that sets up some of the basic problems: the first essay, "Visions of a Biomechanical Apocalypse (First Version)" raises the possibility that one day our Western civilization may crumble into ruins like the shattered Roman Colosseum pictured in Thomas Cole's 1832 painting *Interior of the Colosseum*, or the rubble of antiquity that is so frequently depicted in the art of Frederic Edwin Church. The essay should be regarded, then, as a sort of literary equivalent to one of those paintings, although it takes the perspective of someone from the future looking *back* on the ruins of Technological Civilization.

The second essay, "Ancient Myth and Modern Science" suggests that scientists, when creating theories about the origin and evolution of the universe may be unconsciously drawing upon mythic structures to organize their narratives (a point not original with me, however, for it has been made by William Irwin Thompson and others).[3] But the essay therefore suggests the possibility of a *mythologized science*, one which does not discredit myths but actually returns them to us in a new guise. Indeed, science may one day rescue metaphysics for us from the rubble heap of the collapsed metaphysical age, since the stories brought back from near death survivors, if true, tell of a strange and beautifully luminous Other World that may exist beyond death. Nietzsche's critique of the fable of the "true world" created by humanity as a metaphysical comfort for the sufferings of this one may turn out to have been wrong after all.[4]

The book's second division, "The Pre-Metaphysical Age: From the Neolithic to Ancient Sumer," is composed, likewise, of two essays. The metaphysical age is a concept that was invented by Heidegger,[5] which he demarcated as extending from Plato to Husserl and then theoretician Peter Sloterdijk added his concept of a *pre*-metaphysical age[6] (equivalent to Jean Gebser's mythical consciousness structure), whereas Gianni Vattimo (and others) has mostly worked out the consequences of the *post*-metaphysical age of contemporary modernity.

The first essay of this section, "On the Symbolism of Tools: Hoe and Sickle" sketches out the idea that most tools do not, and have not, originated with pure functionality in mind, but almost always as part of a ritual context controlled by mythological signifieds. Hence, the genealogical line that can be traced from the Acheulean hand axe of *Homo erectus*—too heavy to be of any practical use—to Thor's hammer to the judge's gavel traces out the evolution of the implement from a mythological to a merely secularized juridical context. Mythological signifieds act as controlling ideas on technical implements until their original meanings are forgotten and they are displaced to other contexts, becoming semantically depleted in the process. It is a bit like visiting ancient Hohokam ruins in the Arizona desert, wondering what happened to all the people who once lived there and have now left behind only enigmatic crumbling shells whose meaning and significance are long since forgotten.

13

The second essay in this section tells the story of the tensions between two ancient Sumerian deities, one an agrarian god and inventor of the plough named Ninurta, and the other a patron god of craftsmen named Enki. The chapter describes the battles between these two gods, one from the more northerly city of Nippur and the other from the southernmost city of Eridu, and finds that even back then, more than five thousand years ago, there were tensions between farmers and craftsmen of the towns inside the walls like blacksmiths.

The next section, "The Dawning of the Metaphysical Age," is composed of only one essay, an analysis of the imagery of this book's cover painting by the Dutch Utrecht artist Dirck van Baburen entitled *Prometheus Being Chained by Vulcan.* The deed, as Hesiod makes clear, is an epochal one that brings the Golden Age to a close and inaugurates the rule of Zeus with his victory over the pre-metaphysical age Titans, crowned by his stealing the metaphysical vulva from the Great Mother and giving birth to Athena, goddess of the age of (logocentric) wisdom and rationality that will soon follow. From Athena—who condemns the pre-metaphysical age Furies of matriarchy—to Plato's separation of Being from Becoming through elevation of the Forms to pure transcendence, there is only a short leap. Both are masculinist feats which inaugurate Heidegger's metaphysical age.

The book's final section, "The Post-Metaphysical Age" is composed of four essays: the first is an analysis of the great writer Paul Bowles, who was a sort of tangential member of the Beats, and whose 1949 novel *The Sheltering Sky* was already moving ahead into the post-metaphysical age—just as Mark Rothko's paintings were doing at about the same time[7]—and showing us the consequences of the collapse of the Transcendental Signifieds that once anchored the Western tradition in an age of ritual, myth and philosophical metaphysics. With those signifieds gone, the couple who form the protagonists of the novel find themselves—as do we moderns—adrift, floating across the Saharan desert without aim, purpose or direction only to end up with disastrous consequences (a fable that perfectly describes our contemporary situation).

In the next essay, "Heidegger vs. Coca-Cola," the ancient tradition of the conservative agrarian (or in Heidegger's case, rustic) who *objects* to the technological transformations of modernity are scaled down to two signifiers as metonyms to make the case that not everyone is so enchanted with all these gadgets —which Heidegger calls "mere objects" as opposed to "Things," the former abandoned and cut off from Being while the latter remain anchored precisely *in* Being.[8] Heidegger was one of the first thinkers to warn of the consequences of nihilism and superficiality that such a consumer world—which I have simplified in the essay to the signifier of "Coca-Cola,"—cut adrift from everything local and rooted in meaning and tradition, would bring about.

In the penultimate essay on Ted Kaczynski, the rustic's resentment against Industrial modernity becomes deadly and degenerates from the plane of the Imaginary and the Symbolic back to the zoological violence of the Real that begins, and also ends, every high civilization (*all* of them eventually disappear into a cloud of vaporized signifiers— whether they are "vaporized" by Christian lynch mobs, say, or philosophical extermination, as in the case of the wiping out and absorption of Buddhism in India). Kaczynski tried to play the game first on the plane of the Symbolic with his essay on "Industrial Society and its Future" but did not have the patience or tenacity to learn the craft of writing and go through the agon of finding a market for his ideas. So he resorted to another craft altogether, that of bomb-making, and began mailing bombs to the various men of science whom he saw as the originators of the shallow signifiers of consumer society floating all around us. By deleting those men from existence, he supposed that the source of such signifiers—Coca-Cola, for instance—would simply disappear and Industrial society eventually crumble and collapse in on itself: exactly the vision that I sketched out in this book's opening essay.

The concluding essay, then, comes back full circle—in mythical fashion—with a discussion of Thomas Pynchon's novel *V.*, just as it opens with a brief image from that novel in the inceptual essay. But this time the consequences of the floating signifier known as "V." are fathomed, for Pynchon represents it as a signifier that simply will not stick to *any* Signifieds whatsoever. Herbert Stencil's inability to even verify the existence of the woman "V" is testament to the fact that meaning now in the *post*-post-modern age is nowhere to be found since all signifiers are sliding and skidding free of their signifieds and can therefore be made to refer to *anything whatsoever.*

So, those are the nine or so exhibits that form this author's retrospective glance backwards at a two-decade long career as an American cultural critic in an age when the publishing ecosphere that once enabled such individuals to thrive has simply popped like one of Peter Sloterdijk's macrospheres and disappeared, leaving the individual to become a rogue scavenger foraging for sustenance entirely on his own.

The essays, then, tell two stories: the obvious one is that just outlined above, of the gradual transformation of those Transcendental Signifieds—Derrida's term[9]—once known as the gods into Plato's Forms and the Christian Logos, and then eventually into the philosophical signifieds of philosophers like Kant and Hegel that anchored the metaphysical tradition's last century of existence before it was ruptured by Nietzsche and Heidegger, and then later with French postmodern thought. With the semiotic vacancies left in the Western metaphysical Clearing opened up, ads, icons (in their semantically depleted sense) and commercials instead of Ideas began to "unconceal" themselves from out of the darkness of the Heideggerian woods and to substitute a world of rapidly evanescent signifiers for one anchored in meaning and tradition.

The *other* story told by this retrospective is a disguised autobiography, one that tells the tale of a cultural critic's evolution from the study of comparative mythology to that of Critical Theory and media studies. Unlike most critical theoreticians of today, I began in the field of ritual, symbol and myth—which I studied for about a decade and a half from 1990 to approximately 2005 or so—and then gradually moved out of it when I realized that the field was becoming depleted of ideas and so moved on into the fields of media studies and finally contemporary postmodern philosophy, where ideas were still rich and full of possibilities. I saw that there was much work to be done in combining all three fields—comparative mythology, media studies and continental Critical Theory—to be applied toward an analysis of our contemporary moment.

It has been difficult, however, if not impossible, to make a living doing this sort of thing these days outside the university system—and even there, professors tell me it is becoming more and more difficult to survive *at all*—but at least I have managed to do it, against all advice from friends and family members, for two decades, and have produced 19 books, a website and countless YouTube video lectures as

a result of my stubborn tenacity.
I hope you enjoy the retrospective.

April, 2016 (Mesa, Arizona)

Tensions Between Myth and Science

Visions of a Biomechanical Apocalypse

(First Version)

Thomas Pynchon's Decline of the Flesh

There is an image from Thomas Pynchon's 1963 novel *V.* which I would like to sketch for you. The book's narrative unfolds the story of a quest for the mysterious woman whose first initial forms its title, and as the episodes of the novel concerning her are recounted we discover that she is connected with a series of major political catastrophes that have occurred throughout the course of the 20th century. She was present, for example, as a young 18-year-old at the Fashoda Crisis of Egypt in 1898, which nearly opened a major war between Britain and France. We then find her involved in an anarchist insurrection in Italy that also includes a plot to steal Botticelli's *Birth of Venus* from the Uffizi. She turns up, again, in 1922 as the concubine of a German officer in charge of a genocidal extinction of South African Bondel tribesmen who are in revolt. Finally, we encounter her once more, disguised as a Manichaean priest, on the island of Malta in 1945, where she is apparently killed during a bombing run.

And now here is the image: the woman V. has been pinned beneath an enormous beam knocked loose from the ceiling by an explosion, and when the bombing run has passed, a group of curious children wander into the ruins and discover her. At once, they begin removing the artificial implants and metallic appendages with which, throughout the course of the novel, she has gradually replaced parts of her anatomy. The wig covering her shaven skull is found to conceal a tattoo of the Crucifixion, while her left eye—which they pry forth from its socket—is made of glass and has been painted with a tiny clock face. They also remove the surgically implanted sapphire from her navel, detach her prosthetic feet, and make off with her false teeth, which have been cast out of gold, silver and titanium.

Now, it was Marshall McLuhan who insisted that machines are extensions of human physiology. The printing press, for example, may be thought of as an extension of the eye, or the wheel as an expansion of the foot, or electric circuitry as an amplification of the central nervous system. According to McLuhan, furthermore, each medium not only amplifies the function of the limb that it extends, but also deadens the sensitivities of that very organ. Pynchon's novel, in line with this, suggests that the evolution of technology in the West has resulted in a numbing of our human sensibilities altogether, for V.'s gradual descent into what Pynchon terms "the Inanimate" plays in counterpoint with the unfolding of political violence and chaos during the course of the 20th century. Indeed, Pynchon's novel even suggests that there is an inverse proportion between the "advance" of technology and the dehumanization that tends to accompany it, for we often forget just how much the industry of warfare accelerates technological innovation. Consider, for instance, the rocket, the jet engine, and the computer: these mutations in technological evolution constitute the virtual infrastructure of the Information Age and all were productions of World War II defense industries.

It would seem, then, that the historical paradigm framing Pynchon's vision of the modern world is that of the Western myth of a linear progress of restoration from a fallen state. This particular vision of history as a gradual and inevitable "progress" was first articulated by the Persian prophet Zoroaster, in which the cosmos was pictured at the beginning of Time as a pure world of Light, which then fell into a state of darkened, material corruption, but will one day, through human effort, return to its original purity. This myth has unconsciously fueled all our notions of "progress" and for us moderns it gained a particular significance during the political reforms of the French and American Revolutions of the late 18th century, in which democracy was viewed as an advance over all earlier forms of government.

This political optimism, furthermore, provided fresh impetus to all the cultural domains of the 19th century, especially those of applied science and engineering. The gradual perfection of the steam engine with its mutations, the steamboat and the railroad; its miniaturization in the form of the internal combustion engine; the invention of the dynamo and its applications in the telegraph, electric light, and many other gadgets; such marvels all seemed to refuel the old Zoroastrian-Christian myth of the progress of Man, emerging at last from the darkness of his bondage to nature. The publication in 1859 of Darwin's *Origin of Species* showed that Man had evolved from a state of primitive bestiality and, having proved his fitness in the struggle for supremacy against all other species for domination over the planet, was well on the way to the perfection of human society. And with the publication in the 1890s of James Frazer's multi-volume opus *The Golden Bough* the myth of progress was transplanted to the development of human culture, for in Frazer's view, the "primitive" epochs of magic and religion would eventually be rendered obsolete by the age of science; myth and ritual, therefore, would be forever consigned to the superstitions of man's childhood.

But Frazer couldn't have been more wrong. For the new century dawned with the Great War, and the uses to which these technologies could be put in the service of the mass destruction of human beings was profusely demonstrated. The work of philosophy, furthermore, that best seemed to capture the whole sense of this shifting of historical sensibilities was Oswald Spengler's two-volume work *The Decline of the West* (1918), for Spengler's paradigm, like Pynchon's, was based not upon the myth of linear Progress, but rather on that of the more ancient Bronze Age myth of Eternal Return, in which the phases of history are thought to move in accord with the organic morphology of birth, climax, senescence and death. For Spengler—as for Goethe, Vico and Hesiod before him—each of the great civilizations had demonstrated this, for they were all dead—Vedic India, ancient China, Egypt, the Greeks—and with them had gone their technologies. According to Spengler, a similar fate lay in store for the West. Here, for instance, is his vision of a machine apocalypse from his 1931 treatise *Man and Technics*:

"This machine-technics will end with the [Western] civilization and one day will lie in fragments, forgotten—our railways and steamships as dead as the Roman roads and the Chinese wall, our giant cities and skyscrapers in ruins like old Memphis and Babylon. The history of this technics is fast drawing to its inevitable close. It will be eaten up from within, like the grand forms of any and every Culture. When, and in what fashion, we know not."[10]

And that Spengler's vision was no mere fad made palatable by the catastrophe of the Great War is confirmed by a flood of literary works which followed throughout the course of the 20th century, providing a powerful and seductive counter-player to the 19th century myth of Progress. The first volume of Proust's epic novel *Remembrance of Things Past*, with its elegy for Europe's fading aristocracy, had already appeared in 1913; Yeats's famous poem "The Second Coming" in 1920, followed by his own version of the myth of historical cycles with *A Vision* in 1925; T.S. Eliot's *The Waste Land* in 1922 along with James Joyce's *Ulysses*; Thomas Mann's *The Magic Mountain* in 1924; Arnold J. Toynbee's *A Study of History* and Lewis Mumford's *Technics and Civilization* in 1934; and in 1939, Joyce's final masterpiece *Finnegans Wake* with its vast macro-visions of history always returning the "seim anew," as he puts it in the Anna Livia Plurabelle chapter in which the washerwomen are gossiping as twilight approaches. ("My cold cher's gone ashley," one of them can be heard to mutter in the gloom.)[11]

Viewed through the lens of Spengler's prophecies, then—in which he claimed to be able to be the first to predetermine the fate of a civilization using Goethean morphological principles—Pynchon's image of a cyborg being dismantled by a group of children could be read as an allegory of the coming deconstruction of our biomechanical worldview—and with it, our machines themselves—by future generations. And if Spengler's vision does turn out to be an accurate prophecy of the fate of Western civilization, then the scenario imagined in George Miller's Mad Max films may become actualized on the plane of the Real. In that case, the 19th century myth of linear Progress will fade away and give (re)birth to the older Bronze Age myth of the Eternal Return, wherein the wheel of time must always revolve back toward its ground of origin. In *The Road Warrior*, the Middle Ages return, paradoxically, as our possible future. As the great American poet Robinson Jeffers once put it:

> For someone
> Whispered into my ear when I was very young, some serpent whispered
> That what has gone returns; what has been, is; what will be, was; the future
> Is a farther past; our times he said fractions of arcs of the great circle;
> And the wheel turns, nothing shall stop it nor destroy it, we are bound on the wheel,
> We and the stars and seas, the mountains and the Buddha.[12]

A Vision from the Art of H.R. Giger

There is another image which I would like to sketch for you. In 1979, the science fiction film *Alien* was released, providing a kind of Gothic counterpoint to the optimistic visions of such films as *Star Wars* (1977) and *Close Encounters of the Third Kind* (1977). Science fiction monster films have been around for a long time, and in the 1950s, beneath the radioactive lucence of the post-Manhattan Project era, they gained a particular popularity. But none was so brilliantly executed and beautifully realized as *Alien*, and perhaps no other monster film before it—with the possible exception of *The Exorcist*—was so viscerally disturbing in its imagery of the destruction and breakdown of the human body. *Alien* was the prophecy from a dark oracle, forecasting an ominous glimpse into the disease-infested decade of the 80s, for it managed to convey through the ostensible language of science fiction what was actually the semiotics of another language altogether—that, namely, of viral invasion and cellular destruction.

The visionary genius behind the film was the demon-haunted imagination of Swiss surrealist H.R. Giger, whose images are the descendants of a truly Gothic line of Germanic artists, extending from Hieronymous Bosch and Jakob van Swanenburgh all the way down to Arnold Bocklin. The aliens of the film had sprung from the abysses of Giger's imagination, and perhaps no contemporary artist has better managed to visualize the contours of the biomechanical mythos now in process of working itself out through the productions of our Western poets and artists.

The specific image from *Alien* that I have in mind evokes our Western love for the broken torsos and empty ruins of vanished civilizations, as the crew of the *Nostromo* finds the pilot of an abandoned spaceship whose radio signal they have traced to its source.[13] Inside the ship, they find an enormous interior with curvilinear walls textured more like the densely layered fibrils composing the surface of some bodily organ than the architecture of a spaceship. In the murky silver light pouring in through the oculus of the dome-shaped ceiling, they discern a huge circular dais like a sundial, upon which sits a gigantic being at the controls of a navigational device reminiscent of the telescope of an observatory. The contours of its yellowing skeleton fuse with the chair and surrounding console, as though the being had been genetically engineered to spend its life as the ship's prophetic nucleus, guiding voyages through infinite space with clairvoyant foresight, like those spice-drugged Guild Navigators of Frank Herbert's *Dune* books.

I find this image beautiful and yet disturbing. It reminds me of some of Carl Jung's descriptions in his autobiography, *Memories, Dreams, Reflections*, of dreams involving journeys to mysterious underworlds where strange beings are discovered. In particular, I am thinking of the dream he told of his own childhood, wherein he had gone down through a hole in the earth into a cave, and was terrified to find there a gigantic crowned phallus sitting on a throne. Jung later interpreted this being as an echo of the pagan phallic god Dionysus, lord of wine and sexuality, forgotten since the rise of Christianity, but still slumbering in the collective unconscious of Western civilization, awaiting the day of its return (undoubtedly as Elvis Presley). Then there was the anecdote Jung told of a man who wished to undertake training as a psychoanalyst, and one day told Jung of a dream he had had of getting lost in an abandoned subway, where he followed a set of stairs that led downward into a dark arena where an infant sat in a pool of light smearing itself with its own feces. For Jung, this indicated the presence of a latent psychosis waiting to erupt in the man's psyche, and so he discouraged him from pursuing a career as an analyst.

The centralized presence of these beings in their underworld habitations suggests an isomorphism, to my mind, with the sequence in *Alien* where Giger's space jockey is discovered. It is as though we had undertaken a journey to a level of the collective unconscious of our present Western society and found there a single great image encoding, and compressing, a number of messages for us. One suggests that the giant's biomechanical fusion of machinery and flesh is an index of the state of our present seduction by the wonders of technology: we have become so entranced with its possibilities that we are like cocooned flies caught in a gigantic web, and like the space jockey, we are fated to remain imprisoned at the controls of our great machinery until the vectors of Time have fossilized our bodies, and with them, the imagination of the Western mind.

Giger's paintings, furthermore, are filled with such biomechanical beings and landscapes: convoluted geometries of steel flesh; living topologies of fused chromium and cartilage; strange machines built not of cogs and pistons but of metal bones with sinuous curves and paraboloid arches animated by sentient A.I. beings. Indeed, Giger's paintings are X-rays of the anatomy of our present scientific imagination, in which genetic engineering, plastic surgery, nanotechnology and research into the hybridization of artificial intelligence with the immune system have all conspired to produce a living nightmare of biology trapped like an organelle within the larger structure of all-encompassing machinery. For on the macroscale, we are not only poisoning our rivers with industrial sewage, our skies with CO_2, and our ozone with chlorofluorocarbons, but also our bodies which, as William Irwin Thompson has remarked, "are like pieces of Mulligan stew cooking in a planetary soup of electromagnetic radiation and noise." Links have been established between low frequency radiation and leukemia; and every day we pour bizarre chemistries into our bodies for which they have no evolutionary record and the overloaded immune system, in its effort to sift out information from noise, simply breaks down and begins to dismantle itself. The explosion of hundreds of strange 20th century diseases such as AIDS, spree killers, neuromuscular disorders, neurotransmitter imbalances and the like, suggests that the fusion of machine and flesh may simply result in the destruction of human biology altogether.

The great English poet William Blake said that Eternity was in love with the productions of time, and that was his way of dilating the Incarnation myth to encompass *all* of creation as a manifestation of God. In parallel fashion, I would say that the human organism is in love with its machines, and desires some kind of incarnation within the silicon and metal lattices of systems of Artificial Intelligence such as that pictured by William Gibson in his 1984 novel *Neuromancer*. But it may be precisely this love that draws us—like a bridegroom to his bride, as Augustine said of Christ going to the cross—to our own biomechanical Crucifixion.

David Cronenberg's Body Electric

David Cronenberg is one of the true geniuses working in cinema today, a kind of modern Kafka whose primary thematic concerns have centered around the disintegration of the body and the psyche in our postmodern age. His 1986 film *The Fly* is, in many ways, an updating of Kafka's *Metamorphosis*, but it is his 1983 masterpiece *Videodrome* with which I am concerned here.[14] *Videodrome* is a study of the ideas of Marshall McLuhan, filtered through the lens of the kind of paranoid narrative perfected by Thomas Pynchon in his novel *The Crying of Lot 49*. In Cronenberg's film, a cable television pirate named Max Renn picks up the signal of a show called "Videodrome," which broadcasts snuff violence and pornography. The show was conceived by media prophet Brian O'Blivion—modeled on McLuhan—as the next stage of media evolution. The Videodrome signal, however, is specially designed to create a brain tumor in anyone who watches it, and the tumor itself hijacks the visual cortex in order to project images of violence and sexuality into the fabric of one's waking consciousness. If it is true, as William Irwin Thompson—once again—has remarked, that the "overpoweringly invasive environments of electromagnetic radiation and noise make biological membranes as weak as national boundaries" and result in the breakdown of the immune system, then in Cronenberg's film, the Videodrome brain signal dissolves the membrane that separates waking consciousness from dreaming consciousness, and creates out of one's waking life a protean reality of liquid forms, like those wet watches of Dali's famous painting.

And so the next image which I have in mind is certainly true to the spirit of Surrealist (and even more so, contemporary) art, for as the film's narrative unfolds, Max begins to resemble a piece of living machinery. At one point, an orifice opens up within the center of his torso like some absurd vagina, and in a surrealist parody of the act of intercourse, he "loses" his hand gun inside the orifice, which then seals itself up. Later, Max retrieves the gun from inside his own torso, as though giving birth to this strange mechanical embryo, and in a scene that perfectly captures McLuhan's sense of technology as an extension of the human body, the gun sprouts biomechanical tentacles that burrow into the flesh of his hand and fuse with the bones of his wrist.

But the main image which I am after here occurs when Barry Convex, the CEO of Spectacular Optical—the corporation that has taken over the Videodrome project and murdered Brian O'Blivion—holds up a videocassette and says to Max, "I've got something I want to play for you." Through the cognitive alchemy of Max's hallucinogenic perception, however, the videocassette pulses like some internal organ as the orifice in the center of his torso opens up to receive it. Convex thrusts the cassette into the orifice, and the "program" that it plays is that of an assassin for Spectacular Optical. Max is directed to murder O'Blivion's daughter,

31

who has inherited her father's estate, but in his ontological confusion, he has no idea how much of what he experiences is Videodrome- induced hallucination and how much is real. Ultimately, he self-destructs, and murders everyone whom he believes to be part of the Videodrome conspiracy.

It's the image of that human VCR that interests me here. Is Cronenberg suggesting that we have all become human VCRs in this media-saturated age, just playing back the images which the media inserts in our brains? As Cronenberg has remarked: "The movie goes into the ways in which television does alter us physically. It's what McLuhan was talking about: TV as an extension of our nervous system."

Following McLuhan's and Cronenberg's lead, then, I would like to suggest that images are extensions of the human immune system and are created by the very same biological energies which have built our bodies. And if images in turn may be thought of as the filaments out of which myths are spun, then I would say that the images visualized by our poets and artists compose the substance of our contemporary mythologies, and that these images then correspond to the white blood cells of our cultural immune system.

With the disintegration of our (traditional) cultural immune system, however, the mind becomes susceptible to all manner of psychological viruses, and the media is, of course, the primary means by which they are transmitted. Our cultural immune system, that is to say, is really Tradition itself: the sum total of the ideas and myths out of which the various fabrics of our Western paradigms have been woven. When that body of knowledge is lost or forgotten, as in the case of a Dark Age, the result is the equivalent of a cultural immune deficiency syndrome. When that happens, the psyche becomes prey to all manner of pathological ideas which can distort its development and into the void created by this historical senility, the media then pours the ghostly blue radiance of an artificial past, in which the names and events that have shaped civilizations are replaced by the trivial events of the lives of characters on television shows. When the cast of *Gilligan's Island* or *M.A.S.H.* finally gets to go home, it is an event of (a)historical significance in minds for which the Battle of Actium or the signing of the Magna Carta simply do not exist. Likewise, the 100 pound woman whose self-image has been so badly distorted through cosmetic advertising that she believes she is still somehow "overweight" suffers from a similar pernicious influence.

We are living in an age when imaginary significations are in full disintegration all around us, and caught as we are between two worlds—the one now vanishing and the one yet to emerge (the time of the Between, as Heidegger called it)[15]—*Videodrome* illustrates the ontological confusion and paranoia that can result from the kinds of information overload characteristic of such an age as ours.

Myths, Machines and the Lost Highways of the Future

The mechanistic paradigm created during the 17th and 18th centuries was a vision of the world which made possible the existence of our present technologies—for the internal combustion engine, the turbojet, and the rocket are machines deduced from its most basic principles regarding force, mass and motion. But that paradigm itself has been in full disintegration since the middle of the 19th century, with the rise of thermodynamics and electrodynamics, and then, at the turn of the century, with Relativity and quantum theory. And now with the rise of Chaos theory, Catastrophism and the Gaian earth sciences, incursions from the visionary imagination of mythology seem to be breaking down the mechanical

33

worldview, and along with its collapse may come an inability to make the very machines which that paradigm made possible in the first place.[16] The question of whether these myths will destroy our technologies altogether and leave us with a *Road Warrior* junkyard, or else fuse with them to create a helix of cultural DNA that will spin out new forms of human society remains undecided. Whatever the case may be, however, it is becoming increasingly clear that the old 19th century vision of the future as an endless progression of improving social landscapes in which crime, disease and human religiosity are relegated to the past, has become a lost highway leading to nowhere.

If that is the case, then we today have the rare privilege of living at a moment in history in which the miracles of technology are simply unrivaled in terms of their capabilities. We may even be living in an epoch of human history that will be remembered and idealized in the myths and legends of those to come long after us—as we today still dream of the Greeks of 5th century Athens, or the Italians of the Renaissance. If that be so, then we are participating in the creation of the future myths and dreams of the long line of humans that will pour forth after us over this earth. And they will perhaps regard with wonder, and not a little awe, the structure of our society as they sift through the ruins of our machines and the remnants of our literature, paintings and stories trying to piece together just what it was that happened to us. They will regard us perhaps in the very way those astronauts in *Alien* pondered the ruins of that derelict ship, with its dreaming fossil of a space navigator, wondering what magnificence of imagination it was that could have produced such a civilization.

(1997)

Ancient Myth and Modern Science

Myth as Psychology

Historically, the conflict between myth and science, according to Joseph Campbell, involved a discrediting of visionary cosmology in favor of one based upon "fact." In his essay "The Symbol Without Meaning," Campbell described how science gradually disentangled itself from the mythological projections of the medieval imagination through the discoveries of men like Columbus and Copernicus, which amounted to the "drawing of a distinct dividing line between the world of dream consciousness and that of waking."[17] As a result, "mythological cosmologies...do not correspond to the world of gross facts but are functions of dream and vision,"[18] which means, for Campbell, that myths are projections of the human psyche onto the canvas of the universe. Their validity, consequently, is restricted to the psyche, and all myths are to be regarded as metaphors symbolic of, on the one hand, the mysteries of Being, and on the other, transformations of human consciousness.

Suppose, however, that we discard Campbell's insistence that myths have been cosmologically disqualified by science, and actually read them, instead, in terms of scientific narratives. Is it possible that we may find visions of cosmological knowledge once stored by archaic societies but now rediscovered by modern science?

The Impact of Science Upon Myth

Taking a moment, first, to review in brief sequence the impact of the various scientific revolutions upon the Biblical imagination of the cosmos may give us, like Petrarch standing atop Mount Ventoux, a sense of perspective.

During the Middle Ages, the cosmos was thought to be a kind of immense Gothic cathedral composed of three storeys: Heaven, Hell and the Earth, which latter, because of its weight, was at the furthest remove from the divine. Dante situated his Inferno inside the core of the Earth, with Satan having plunged like a comet into its center, where he hung, bat-like, upside down, while the entire southern hemisphere was made up of a massive ocean within which the mountain of Purgatory rested as a lone island, and at the top of which Eden, with its four rivers, poured out its inexhaustible wellsprings. The cosmos itself had unfolded as part of a three act drama of Genesis, Crucifixion and Apocalypse which, in contradistinction to the cyclic visions of the Greeks and the Hindus, was to be regarded as a unique, and never to be repeated, occurrence.

Beginning in 1492 with the discoveries of Columbus, however, the old T and O maps of the earth had to be redrawn as a fourth continent was added to those of Africa, Europe and Asia (comprising the shape of the "T"), and the centering of cosmic order on Jerusalem, which had been the axial bull's eye of medieval maps, now shifted to the coastal cities of Spain and Italy with their newly emerging commercial powers in which the natural scientist and the bourgeois merchant had come to replace the priest and the king as worldly authorities. Half a century later, with Copernicus in 1543, the heavens had to be revisioned and another old medieval center, that of the earth, was relocated to that of the sun.

With the articulation of his clockwork cosmos, Newton surgically removed the angels from their spheres with the scalpel of the infinitesimal calculus, for the motion of the planets no longer required the agency of occult forces, but could perfectly well be explained on the twin principles of inertia and gravitation. By the eighteenth century, Immanuel Kant and Laplace had given a convincing explanation for the origin of the solar system with their hypothesis of a spinning cloud of dust and gas slowly condensing into the sun and planets. Accordingly, when Napoleon asked him where God fit into his celestial mechanics, Laplace famously replied, "Sire, I have no need of *that* hypothesis."

Near the end of the eighteenth century, with James Hutton's uniformitarian theory of the slow, phlegmatic origin of the earth's geosphere, evidence was beginning to amass in favor of an evolutionary theory of the origin of the earth's crust over inconceivably vast epochs of glacial time, thus burying once and for all Bishop Ussher's date for God's creation of the earth in 4004 BC. And with the publication in 1830 of Lyell's *Principles of Geology*, the uniformitarian theory became a dogma of the church of science, thus giving Darwin the sacred text that he needed—and which he took with him aboard the *Beagle*—to build his theory of evolution by natural selection, which required a temporal canvas of hundreds of millions of years. Thus, there was no longer any necessity to assume that species had been stamped out by God at the beginning of creation like molds at a steel-works factory.

With the simultaneous creations of the theory of Relativity and quantum mechanics at the turn of the century, new horizons of the mind and imagination opened up, for not only had the impacts of science destroyed the crumbling edifice of the mythology of Christianity, but now it began to dissolve the mechanistic cosmos itself. Einstein melted down time and space and extracted from their ore the incandescent vision of a single humming, mass-energy field from out of which the planets and stars had emerged as particularly dense concentrations of energy. The tiny—yet also immense—interior of the atom, meanwhile, had begun to reveal its hitherto unsuspected qualities in which quantum events replaced causal ones.

The dizzying speeds and vast infinitudes of the picture of the universe bequeathed to us by the Einsteinian revolution has rendered the once mighty creation myth of the Bible a merely provincial vision of a group of desert tribesmen wandering over the hills of Judea. As Joseph Campbell—once again—points out in "The Symbol Without Meaning," the very speed of light itself has rendered any theory of the bodily resurrection of Christ absurd, since even if he had ascended at the speed of light, he would not yet be out of our galaxy, the Milky Way, which is about 100,000 light years across. Our own solar system is located near one of the spiral tips about 30,000 light years from the center. The crucifixion of Christ 2,000 years ago is simply not enough time for any kind of physical ascension to have taken place.[19]

And so, the impact of science upon the transcendental signifieds of the Bible has all but demolished that world. Mythology, accordingly—no longer entangled with our cosmological image of the world—has withdrawn into the psyche, and so all of myth became, as far as Carl Jung and Joseph Campbell were concerned, a projection of the human psyche onto the canvas of the cosmos. With nowhere now for the projections to go, they have gone inward, for mythology, according to Campbell, "is psychology misread as cosmology, history or biography."[20]

But perhaps there is more to myth, after all, than mere psychology.

Micromyths (or the Impact of Myth Upon Science)

In the *Brihadharanyaka Upanishad*, there is recounted the myth of the Great Self whose cosmic loneliness is so immense that it splits into two beings, the first man and the first woman. The woman, trying to hide from the man who is now her husband, changes herself into a cow, but the husband then transforms himself into a bull, and together they produce all the cattle. Then she turns into a mare, he into a stallion; she into a female donkey, he into a male donkey, and so on until all the animals are produced. Finally, the husband has a revelation when he realizes that all the phenomena of the world have come forth from himself. "I alone am the creation," he concludes, "for I created all this."[21]

The Hindu image of the cosmos as the body of a single living Being is a vision sprung from the depths of thousands of years of yogic practice, going back, perhaps, as far as Harappa and Mohenjo Daro. Indeed, the entire civilization, in contrast with the West, has been inward turned all along, as a comparison of the eye-motifs of Hindu sculpture with those of the Greeks reveals, for the eyes of the gods and heroes of Indian art are usually closed, whereas those of the West are wide open. I would like to suggest that this particular

39

creation myth—and there are, of course, thousands of them in Hindu sacred literature—*might* be rooted in a visionary transformation of cellular mitosis that came to some *rishi* while in trance (what is known as a "proprioception," in other words). Mitosis is the process whereby living forms grow, as one cell splits into two, two into four and so on. This organic movement from center to periphery, and from less form to more, would then be a *deep structure* shared by the Hindu creation myth with Western scientific knowledge.

In his book *The Body of Myth*, physicist J. Nigro Sansonese develops his thesis that all "myth describes a systematic exploration of the human body by the privileged members of archaic cultures."[22] Myths, according to Sansonese, are encoded descriptions of physiological processes envisioned by yogis and shamans in trance states. He describes, for example, how the myth of Perseus slaying the Kraken by showing it the head of Medusa and turning it to stone is actually a description of the stopping of the heart along the vagus nerve that connects it to the visual centers at the back of the brain. The monster with all its tentacles is the vagus nerve itself, while the head of the Medusa with its snakes is "a description of the brain and its twelve cranial nerves."[23] And the entire story, then, describes how the yogi stops the beating of his own heart while in *samadhi*.

If Sansonese's theory is correct, then a deep structure shared by the Hindu creation myth with the process of cellular mitosis might in fact exist. If it is possible that visualizations of interior physiological processes can become manifest to yogis in trance states, then it is certainly worth considering that the Hindu creation myth is, on one level anyway, a visualization of a somatic process.

The same goes for shamanic trance states, as Jeremy Narby describes in his elegant book *The Cosmic Serpent*. Narby is an ethnobotanist who wondered whether it could be true, as Amazonian tribesmen claimed, that their extensive botanical knowledge originated in trance states induced by *ayahausca*, a psychoactive infusion derived from an Amazonian vine. The more he thought about the structural isomorphism shared by the double helix of DNA with the images of snakes and ladders universal to shamanism, the more he began to suspect that the serpents and geometrical patterns of shamanic iconography might actually be proprioceptions of DNA and intracellular activity. In the book, Narby details a series of paintings inspired by ayahausca visions that he showed to a friend conversant with molecular biology. His friend identified the geometric patterns as unraveled DNA, chromosomes during specific phases of mitosis, triple helix collagen structures and so on.[24] In other words, Narby discerned the deep structures shared by shamanic trance visions with scientific knowledge of the soma. Thus, perhaps, Western civilization has arrived at knowledge by way of technological extensions of sensory organs that tribal peoples have long ago arrived at through proprioceptions during meditation and trance.

There exists, as a final example, a tradition in Christian mysticism of visionary states in which angels descend to human beings in order to inspire them with the spirit, as in the Annunciation, in which the angel Gabriel descends to announce to Mary that she is to become *Theotokos*, or "God-bearer." In most illustrations of this myth during the Middle Ages, Gabriel's descent is accompanied by a miniature dove—signifier of the Holy Spirit—and the power of the Word, the Logos itself, is rendered visible entering into Mary's ear. Thus, Mary is impregnated by the power of the Word, and her response is to say, "My soul doth magnify the Lord."

But now consider the isomorphism of this with the image of a virus landing on a cell wall. The virus attaches itself and then squirts into the cell its own DNA—or RNA, as the case may be—which then overtakes the cell's normal replicating functions and forces it to copy this new program, whereupon it then spits out hordes of viruses which burst through the cell and move on to other conquests. I am reminded here of a miniaturized version of the Annunciation from an illuminated manuscript by Fra Angelico (below) which depicts a historiated initial capital "R," in which the Virgin Mary sits below the leg of the R, while Gabriel hovers just outside it. Immediately above her, in the R's rounded oval, God the Father sits, gazing down, while from his fingertips the luminous golden sheen of the Logos extends, with the dove at its tip, puncturing through the arch of the "R" as though it were a cellular membrane separating Mary—who sits below like a blue nucleus—from God and the angel Gabriel.

The image of a virus landing on a cell wall and squirting its DNA into the nucleus is isomorphic with Fra Angelico's illustration—although this may be a mere accident of the syntactical grammar shared by such images—but it is important to point out that the metaphysical and spiritual implications of the myth are in no way reduced to a biological function. Whereas a Jungian reading, for example, would elucidate precisely those dimensions through a cross-cultural comparison of the Virgin Birth with, say, the impregnation of the Buddha's mother by a tiny white elephant—or the myth of the birth of the monkey king Hanuman from the semen of Shiva poured by sages into the ear of Hanuman's mother, Anjani—the point of *this* exercise is rather to develop new organs of perception with which to view ancient myths in a way that sidesteps the dogma of a Jungian approach.

It is important to point out that the metaphysical and spiritual implications of myth are in no way reduced to a biological function by these examples. If Narby and Sansonese are right, then the realization of these mythic images as micromyths of cellular processes should induce us to study myths in a new way, for it will be seen that, contrary to our historical introduction, science does *not* render myth obsolete, but rather that myth impacts science in a new way.

Macromyths

One of the primary functions of mythology—what Campbell used to call its "cosmological function"—is to project a world picture onto the universe that is consistent with the knowledge of the time. The Christian cosmographer Cosmas, for example, in the 6th century AD imagined that the universe was a sort of gigantic chest in which the sun and moon revolved around a single enormous mountain that stood up like a monolith from out of a flat earth surrounded by water. Of course, the Greeks had long since deduced the rotundity of the earth, and had even drawn up rough draft sketches of the theory of evolution and the heliocentric hypothesis, both of which were discarded, just as the primordial Christians discarded the world image of the Greeks since, in both cases, the images clashed with the respective spiritual dispositions of each culture.

Today we look to science for our knowledge of what the universe looks like, and when we turn to examine certain scientific narratives of the origins of things with an eye for the deep structures that these narratives might have in common with ancient myths, we find surprising parallels. An example is the current scientific story of the creation of the universe. The idea of what has come to be known as the Big Bang was first put forth by a Catholic priest, the Abbe Georges Lemaitre, who in 1927 suggested that the universe might have arisen from a sort of "primal atom" of matter and energy. The idea of the emergence of the universe from a cosmic egg is, however, a mythological one as well, found all over the world. Here is another creation myth, this one from the *Chandogya Upanishad* (3.19):

"In the beginning this world was simply what is non-existing; and what is existing was that. It then developed and formed into an egg. It lay there for a full year and then it hatched, splitting in two, one half becoming silver and the other half gold. The silver half is this earth while the golden half is the sky."[25]

This, meanwhile, is from a Tibetan creation myth:

"From the essence of the five primordial elements a great egg came forth...Eighteen eggs came forth from the yolk of that great egg. The egg in the middle of the eighteen eggs, a conch egg, separated from the others. From this conch egg, limbs grew, and then the five senses, all perfect, and it became a boy of such extraordinary beauty that he seemed the fulfillment of every wish..."[26]

And finally an Orphic creation myth from ancient Greece:

"...black-winged Night, a goddess of whom even Zeus stands in awe, was courted by the Wind and laid a silver egg in the womb of Darkness; and...Eros, whom some call Phanes, was hatched from this egg and set the universe in motion."[27]

Thus Lemaitre, when describing his theory of the origin of the universe from a cosmic egg, may have been subconsciously drawing from a mythological image. Then there is the deep structure shared by ancient creation myths with current narratives of the origins of life on this planet. On the first page of his book *The Fifth Miracle: The Search for the Origin and Meaning of Life*, physicist Paul Davies describes two contrasting theories regarding the origins of the first microbes. The old idea of cells emerging on the surface of the ocean in the presence of sunlight (and lightning), he insists, is made obsolete by new evidence, for "it now appears that the first terrestrial organisms lived deep underground, entombed within geothermally heated rocks in pressure cooker conditions. Only later did they migrate to the surface."[28] Several pages further on, he says that "our eldest ancestors did not crawl out of the slime so much as ascend from the sulfurous underworld."[29]

Now as anyone familiar with Native American myth knows, the common narrative for the origins of life involved the myth of emergence from the underworld. It is particularly widespread amongst the tribes of the Southwest—for example, the Hopi, whose famous kivas are miniaturizations of this underworld. In a Navaho myth, the first people are in danger of being drowned by a flood, and as the waters rise, they and all the other animals climb onto a gigantic reed that grows up to the world ceiling, from whence the First Man digs his way through to this, the upper world, in which we are presently dwelling.

On the same page, Davies suggests an exactly opposed theory for the origins of life, and, along with it, invokes an equally opposite mythological cosmogony when he says that life may have been brought *to* the earth *from* the heavens by meteorites from Mars that may have crashed into its Hadean oceans.[30] The deep structure here is isomorphic with the creation myth of the Sky Father, one example of which is found on the first page of the Book of Genesis, in which Yahweh infuses the watery abyss with the Spirit. That image, in turn, was embedded in an older Mesopotamian cosmology that associated the heavens with the realm of the gods and the earth with clay that required an external agency from above to give it form.

In her book *Narratives of Human Evolution*, bioanthropologist Misia Landau examines a series of accounts of hominization from Darwin to Leakey and discovers that they all have in common the hidden narrative pattern of the hero myth. Using Vladimir Propp's *Morphology of the Folktale* as a stencil, she makes visible within these so-called "objective" narratives the presence of the hero myth as described in folk tales. According to Propp, the formula is of a humble hero who departs on a journey, receives magical aid from a donor figure, survives a series of tests and trials and arrives at some sort of an apotheosis. Landau shows how, in scientific narratives of human evolution, the hero is the nonhuman primate who departs from his arboreal habitat with the aid of natural selection and who is tried and tested by competition from other animals, harsh climate and predation, but eventually arrives at an apotheosis in the achievement of the upright posture of humanity.[31]

Upon examining scientific narratives of three key points in the quest for the origins of things—of the cosmos, of life upon the earth, and the emergence of the human from the animal—we discover structural isomorphisms with the ancient myths of the cosmic egg, emergence from the underworld, creation from the heavens and the hero myth. Apparently, then, scientists are mythologizing a lot more often than they realize when giving us their accounts of the origin and evolution of all things earthly.

It is probable that we will never know precisely what "happened" at these key points in the evolution of the cosmos, because they involve knowledge of something that transcends the capacity of the human intellect ever to grasp. For whenever we pose such questions as "Who are we? Where do we come from? Where are we going?" we are postulating eternal questions that can be answered only in terms of the complex semiotics of myth. When the human mind goes in search of origins, it strains its limits and begins to crack, while myth comes rushing along to fill in the gap. Perhaps Immanuel Kant was right: we cannot know the world as it is in itself, but only through the human mind's mythological schemata, for between ourselves and "reality" the screen of myth always structures our perceptions.

(2002)

The Pre-Metaphysical Age: From the Neolithic to Ancient Sumer

On the Symbolism of Tools:

Hoe and Sickle

On the Genealogy of the Hoe-as-Phallus

Whenever we trace the history of this or that gadget back far enough, we inevitably find that its earliest origins began in the realm of myth and religion, rather than in practical utility. The umbrella, for instance, did not begin as a device for keeping rain and sun away, but rather originated as a symbol of the world center which always accompanied kings, indicating that it was he himself who incarnated the *axis mundi*.[32] The earliest mirrors—made of polished obsidian—are found as part of grave regalia accompanying females at Catalhoyuk; metallurgy began during the Pottery Neolithic, not for the making of weapons and tools, but rather as an art of crafting jewelry for personal adornment; and there is evidence that the earliest pottery vessels—too small and delicate for cooking—were used for ritual lustrations.

Consider, likewise, the two most important tools used in primitive agriculture: the hoe and the sickle. They are among the earliest farming instruments invented (both originated with the Natufians of Mesolithic Palestine) and their original symbolism was thoroughly cosmological, implying the fundamental dualism of the agricultural process, that namely, of sowing and reaping, or Sex and Death.

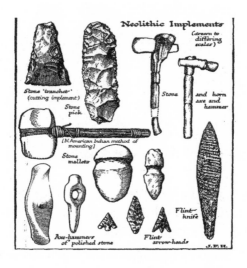

The hoe was invented by the late Natufians somewhere around 10,000 BC, and its basic form suggests a genealogy leading back to the very much more ancient Acheulean hand axe of the Lower Paleolithic (an epoch spanning from about 3.4 million to 300,000 years ago), itself perhaps symbolic of the thunderbolt which fells trees.[33] Tapering to a point at the hafted end with a kind of large tang, the other end, the business end, was semi-circular and would have been used for breaking up the soil prior to sowing. The wooden hafts, of course, have not survived, but the head was made from flaked flint and indeed, this design was so basic that it remained essentially unchanged for three thousand years, since hoes of identical size, shape and material were found amongst the remains of Hassunan cultures in northern Mesopotamia.

Symbolically speaking, the hoe is the "phallic" principle which breaks open the earth so that it can be seeded. Ancient cosmogonic myths confirm this: in the early Sumerian story known as "The Song of the Hoe," for example, the god Enlil is said to have separated the heavens from the earth so that the seed could sprout up from the field.[34] Then he created the first hoe and drove it into the earth, opening a furrow from out of which the first human beings emerged. Thus, like the Native Americans of the Southwestern United States, the Sumerians, too, had an emergence myth, in which the first people were born from the ground like plants. The hoe cracks open the soil so that the seed can be dropped into it, and this essentially erotic symbolism is later taken over by the plough, as a glance at the Sumerian "Theogony of Dunnu" confirms. In this myth, Plough marries Earth and together they break up the virgin soil of the land; from out of the furrow thus made is born the Sea. Then, mysteriously, the narrative reverts to a parthenogenetic myth, for the next line says, "The Furrows, *of their own accord*, begot the Cattle God."[35] (italics mine). The results are similar to Hesiod's *Theogony*: the Cattle God ends up marrying his mother the Earth and killing his father Plough.

In Greek mythology, the lord of the plough was a figure known as Triptolemos ("thrice-plowed"), who was said to be the first king whom Demeter taught the arts of agriculture. He was also the first man to be initiated into the Eleusinian mysteries. Once he had learned the art of agriculture, Demeter put him into a chariot pulled by two flying serpents and let him loose to spread the gospel to mankind. In representations of Triptolemos on vase paintings, moreover, he sometimes appears standing with one hand grasping his plough, with the plough represented in such a way that its handle becomes a clear visual pun of a phallus.[36] In ancient Egypt, the god Min was the lord of agriculture, and he was depicted standing upon a pedestal with an erect phallus and one raised arm holding a flail. The symbol of the nome of Coptos, moreover, which Min ruled, was the thunderbolt, and so we may guess that there was an analogy between the thunderbolt striking the earth and the phallus of Min as the plough digging furrows into it.

Thus, from the Acheulean hand axes made by *Homo erectus* in the Lower Paleolithic to the stone hoes of Natufian man in the Mesolithic, and on down to the plough of the Pottery Neolithic, there is a direct line of symbolic descent in which a tool incarnating the heavenly thunderbolt as a seminal, masculine force striking the earth is developed.

However, it is worth noting that in Egypt, the sexual valencies of heaven and earth were the opposite of those almost everywhere else—for there the sky was a goddess, Nut, and the earth a god, Geb—so that the symbolism of the hoe breaking open the ground did not have the same sexual connotations as elsewhere. Consequently, to break open the earth with a hoe was not analogized to a sexual act, but rather to a post-mortem resurrection ritual known as the Opening of the Mouth, in which an adze was used to symbolically open the mouth of the deceased, having the magical effect of reanimating his subtle body, so that he could defend himself in the afterlife by pronouncing spells to keep demons away. The Opening of the Mouth was modeled upon the opening of the newborn child's mouth, and the clearing out of the mucus so that it could breathe, eat and live. The ceremony was thus associated with the bestowal of life. Furthermore, in Egypt both the adze and the hoe were similarly shaped, as though to imply a deliberate analogy between cutting a furrow into the earth and opening the mouth of a dead person to prepare him for rebirth in the Afterlife. Hence, in the *Pyramid Texts* we find utterances like these: "The earth is hacked up by the hoe, the offering is presented. . .the two nomes of the god shout before [the King] when he goes down into the earth. O Geb, open your mouth for your son Osiris…" (PT, Utt. 560)[37] Or, even more to the point: "The mouth of the earth is split open for this King, Geb has spoken to him." (Utt. 548)[38]

In the classical world, likewise, there is an image of a god whose open mouth forms a portal to the underworld, for in Ovid's *Metamorphoses,* the defeated giant Typhon is depicted in such a way that his mouth is aligned with the volcano Etna in Sicily, which occasionally spews forth flames, for Typhon was a fire-breathing serpent-man whom Zeus had overthrown prior to his assumption of kingship. Curiously, Ovid's version is the only one that describes Typhon pinned down by four mountains in a posture that is suggestive of a crucifixion, with Typhon's right hand pinned down by Mount Pelorus, his left by Pachynus, while both legs together "are in Mount Lilybaeum's grasp." His head is pressed down by Mount Etna.[39] Since Ovid lived exactly during the time in which Christ was crucified, one wonders about his choice of depicting Typhon as the victim of a crucifixion, since one of the esoteric interpretations of Christ pinned to the cross is that of a son returned to his mother's body (for the cross is symbolic of the earth, as in Greek philosophy, where it symbolized the four elements).

Typhon had been born from the earth parthenogeneti-cally—that is to say, without insemination by a male—in two different accounts. According to the most famous one, he was born when Gaia, angered by Zeus's defeat of the Gi-ants (or, in some accounts, the Titans) coupled with Tarta-rus to give birth to Typhon in a cave, but since Tartarus is actually the underworld, Gaia is more or less fecundating herself, and so this myth is a modified parthenogenesis. But in another early text, the "Homeric Hymn to Apollo," his parthenogenesis is more direct, for there it is stated that Ty-phon was born from Hera when she became jealous of Ze-us's parthenogenetic birth of Athena from his head, for she was dissatisfied with her earlier attempt at parthenogenesis with the smith god Hephaestus.[40] Accordingly, Aeschylus in his *Prometheus Bound* portrays Typhon as pinned beneath Mount Aetna while "on the peak Hephaestus hammers red-hot iron."[41]

The Sickle: a Toothed Vagina?

The story of the clash between Zeus and Typhon is impor-tant for the light that it sheds on the relationship between agriculture and myths of monster slayings. In the account given by Apollodoros, Zeus takes a swing at Typhon with a flint sickle, the very same flint sickle—according to Robert Graves—which was used by his father Kronos to separate Ouranus from Gaia.[42] Several monsters in Greek myth are disposed of by sickles: Perseus, for instance, uses a sickle to cut off the head of Medusa, while Heracles is given a sickle by his companion Iolaus to cut off the heads of the Lernaean hydra. All three monsters, moreover, are the offspring of the earth, either directly, as in the case of Typhon and Medusa, or indirectly, as in the case of the hydra who is the offspring of Typhon and Echidna. Since we know that sickles were invented for the purpose of cutting down grain, we may suspect that some kind of agrarian analogy to reaping lies somewhere behind these myths. No better image of cutting grain stalks could be asked for, perhaps, than that of the Lernaean hydra's heads which, once cut down, grow right back.

Now, the sickle, (above) like the hoe, was also invented by the Natufians, who made them from the bones of ruminants with flint flakes set into them like teeth in a jawbone, and ornamented one end of them with the heads of herbivores—aurochs or gazelle—like the atlatls of the hunters of the Upper Paleolithic. (Note that the technique of harvesting is still being expressed through the earlier form language of the animals that had composed the very cosmos of Paleolithic man. In this respect, the Natufian sickles are an example of McLuhan's principle of new technologies being expressed through the language of an older technology.). But the similarity to a jawbone may not have been accidental, for the animal head ornamentation at the tip of the sickle implies that just as the ruminant eats grass, so does the sickle cut down the wheat. Sickles, furthermore, are usually crescent-shaped, which suggests an analogy to the moon, for the moon, like grain, is endlessly cut down but yet grows back. In classical representations of the Greek god Kronos, an intended analogy between sickle and moon is unmistakable, for the shape of his sickle replicates that of the crescent moon precisely. In the Middle Ages, the sickle is traded out for the scythe, but the thanatological symbolism is the same, for both the allegorical figures of Death and Father Time—originally modeled upon Kronos—are equipped with scythes, as Erwin Panofsky has shown in his *Studies in Iconology*.

That the sickle was in its origin thought to be analogous to a lower jawbone—and hence to part of a skull, thus reinforcing its linkage with death—is confirmed by a glance at Hesiod's *Theogony*, where the sickle used by Kronos to castrate his father is described as either "sharp-toothed" or else "full of teeth."[43] This is no mere hyperbole since it is common knowledge amongst myth scholars that Hesiod's *Theogony* borrowed from an older Hittite theogony known as the "Myth of Kumarbi," in which the castration of the sky father—in this case, Anu—occurs when Kumarbi actually *bites off* his genitals. Hence, the appropriateness of the scythe as an attribute of the Grim Reaper, for the sickle was originally envisioned as a mouth full of teeth and the Reaper was normally depicted with a skull for a head.

Already by the period which succeeded that of the Natufians, known as the Pre Pottery Neolithic A (9500 – 8700 BC), the symbolism of the sickle was becoming semantically depleted, for at sites like Aswad in the Damascus oasis and at Mureybet on the Euphrates, sickles began to appear with a single, long flint blade (instead of multiple flint microliths) that would have made it a more efficient cutting instrument. But the replacement of multiple microflints with one blade is tantamount to a loss of the original conception of the sickle as analogous to a mouthful of teeth, and so here we have one of the earliest examples of an improvement in technology occurring at the expense of a controlling mythological symbolism.

At any rate, whereas the hoe had erotic connotations, the sickle was thanatological. While the hoe was a transformation of the Acheulean hand axe and made out of stone, sickles were made out of bone, horn or wood (with the exception of the flint teeth). Sometimes the bones were aurochs ribs, sometimes antler's horns, but they were always taken from herbivores, never carnivores, for carnivores do not eat grass, and the sickle was always meant to connote a mouth chewing cereal grains. The origins of the hoe, on the other hand, may have originally linked it to the idea of a thunderbolt, for the Paleolithic axe is a forerunner of the later greenstone axe—invented at the same time as the single bladed sickle—which is meant to be symbolic of the thunderbolt hurled by the storm god at the mighty oak trees.

Myth and Technology

Technology, then, was originally controlled by symbolic and mythological thinking. For ancient humanity, absolutely every process that we moderns associate with the banalities of daily life—cooking, eating, even cleaning—had a symbolic analogy. For no matter how practical the process, by drawing symbolic analogies in mythological terms, the mind is kept constantly in touch with the spirit world, and hence woven into it in such a way that there is no separation between the physical and the spiritual, or between nature and the gods. Such an opposition between the two realms is common to our thinking because we live today in the shadow of a post Jewish-Zoroastrian vision of the Fall of matter from the world of light. Such a separation has been necessary, perhaps, for the destiny of the West and its appointed mastery over the physical plane, but the cost of this development has been an impoverishment of the human imagination and a degradation of the realm of the gods.

When we think of technology, we think primarily of tools and machines which are used for accomplishing a task or a process. All we require to hammer this particular nail is a heavy object with a metal head. The idea of there being a symbolism involved with the hammer is something that we think would merely get in the way of the task or slow it down in order that some god first be invoked, or some ritual involved that would complicate the process with unnecessary taboos. After all, time is precious and we are interested only in getting things *done*. There is money to be made, and the faster things can be put together—in the largest quantities—the quicker and larger the amounts of money that will come flowing back. Hence, in a society built around capitalism and industry, money comes first, ideas come—if at all—later.

Meanwhile, the stripping of symbolism from our tools and machines does not go ahead without consequences, whether we are willing to heed them or not. For we forget that these very tools and devices which are made for a purpose actually demand to be *used*, for as Neil Postman liked to point out, to a man with a hammer in his hand, everything looks like a nail. Stripped of a controlling symbolism, the machines then turn back around on *us* and begin to dictate *their* purposes to our consciousness. Before we know it, we soon find ourselves in the midst of their captivity, having become merely slaves to their functions. Hence, the science fictional premises of some of our modern films like *The Matrix* or *Dark City*, in which human beings are harvested by machines and forced to perform tasks that are essentially dehumanizing are visualizations, in imagistic language, of our current situation. It is not an accident that these scenarios come up so often in our popular movies and novels, for the human imagination is a living thing with its own purposes and ideas, and it is trying to communicate to us that we are in trouble psychologically, for we are at the mercy of our mechanical environments.

So the early tools of primordial man were mythological ideas incarnate. The Idea precedes the invention, and makes it possible. Culture, therefore, is shaped not by economics, but by ideas. It is only later on, in decadent phases of societies when tools have become semantically depleted of meaning that they become merely practical devices without references beyond their mere function, as is the case today. When that happens, technology takes control of the culture, and the human imagination shrivels up and dies.

(2005)

The Farmer Against the Blacksmith:

Regarding Some Ancient Sumerian Myths

Prologue

In the first few minutes of William Friedkin's 1973 horror film *The Exorcist*, Father Merrin, who is working as an amateur archaeologist on a dig at the ancient Assyrian city of Nineveh in Northern Iraq, is shown seated at an outdoor café. He is sick and trembling, and after taking a few pills, he seems to stabilize, but the sound can be heard ringing constantly in the background of three blacksmiths hammering away at an implement in their nearby forge. Merrin—who has just recently dug up an amulet of the head of the demon Pazuzu (which was worn by pregnant Assyrian women as a pendent around the neck to ward off evil spirits from attacking their unborn children)—stops for a moment as he passes the forge where the three smiths are busy hammering at their glowing implement. They pause to take a break in the heat, and one of them turns to look at Merrin as he wipes his brow, showing the viewer that his right eye has gone a pale, nacreous white. Merrin, slightly unnerved by this apparition of the "evil eye," then moves on to continue with the business of examining his finds.

But the interesting thing to note about the scene is the association of the blacksmith with a debility of some kind—in this case, a blind eye—since smiths all throughout the history of mythology have been associated with wounds, scars and limps: a trait marking them as untrustworthy, flawed and always somehow corrupt. The Cyclopes in Hesiod's *Theogony*, for instance, who make Zeus's weapons for him are all one-eyed; Hephaestus, in Greek myth, was born deformed, which caused Hera to cast him out of Olympus; and Wieland the Smith in the *Poetic Eddas* was eventually hamstrung by the king so that he could not escape and had to invent a pair of wings to fly away from his captivity on an island.

My analysis of the following Sumerian tale of "The Exploits of Ninurta" will conclude by suggesting that the so-called Asag demon which the warrior hero Ninurta kills, just *might* be the oldest blacksmith ever to appear in the history of literature. It is all the more fitting, then, that the story takes place in roughly the same part of the world as Father Merrin on his dig in Nineveh, although it is set a couple of thousand years earlier than the Neo-Assyrian empire which was destroyed in the seventh century BC by the Babylonians, the Persians and the Medes.

Ninurta and the Asag Demon

In the Sumerian tale known variously as "The Exploits of Ninurta" or the *Lugale*, we are in the presence of one of the oldest monster-slayer stories on record. The text as we have it now dates probably from the time of King Gudea of Lagash

(c. 2141 – 2122 BC),[44] that is to say, roughly twenty or thirty years after the collapse of the Akkadian empire (c. 2160 BC) which was invaded by a swarm of barbarians known as Gutians, and indeed, the text contains certain anxieties regarding the barbarian hordes of the Zagros mountains to the east and northeast. South of where the Gutians had originated lay the old adversary of the Sumerians, the Elamites, who—together with the Amorites—eventually overthrew the Third Dynasty of Ur and carried off its last king, Ibbi-Sin (c. 1940 BC) as captive; while to the north of the Gutians was located a group of people known as the Lullubi, one of the great enemies of the Akkadians. To the northwest, extending into the region of the Taurus mountains in Anatolia, there were the Hurrians, and directly west were the tribes of the Amorites (who would later become the Babylonians). Thus, the Sumero-Akkadian empire was surrounded by a crescent of barbarian peoples, each of which lay waiting for its moment to enter the stage of world history and carry off the spoils from Mesopotamia.

So when we turn to the story of "The Exploits of Ninurta,"[45] it is clear that the topmost stratum, as it were, is an historical allegory of the Sumerian peoples fighting the barbarians who constantly poured in from the surrounding mountain ranges. On the face of it, then, the story is a recounting of how the god Ninurta (known also as Ningirsu)[46]—the son of Enlil (who was the inventor of the hoe, whereas Ninurta was associated with the invention of the plough and irrigation)[47]—went to war against the Asag demon from the mountains, a demon who led an army of stone soldiers against him, and how Ninurta overthrew them and, in the process, invented irrigation.

But since mythology is polyphonic and not monophonic, it is able to carry multiple harmonic lines of meaning and

play them off against each other in simultaneous counterpoint. Myths are neither mathematical equations, nor are
they merely ciphers translated into a code and directed only
at those who know how to crack the code. They are much
richer and more texturally dense than that, for they are capable of storing many levels of knowledge in multi-dimen-
sional ways, which is why they are ideally suited to transmit
information across millennia. And so, when we look at the
story of Ninurta and Asag from the point of view of comparative mythology, we find that it is like a hyperdimension-
al sphere that can be turned now this way, now that, each
direction unlocking a new level of knowledge and meaning
that transcends the literalism of the mere codecracker.

In the story, Ninurta—whose name, significantly, may
mean "Lord Plough,"[48]—has no sooner taken up his throne
than his magical weapon, a lion-headed mace known as
the *Shar-ur,* begins warning him that a mighty ruler is aris-
ing to the north, the Asag demon, who is leading an army
of stone soldiers over the mountains. Asag is described as
"deformed"[49] and Ninurta decides that he must go to war
against this creature, which will be the twelfth in a series
of monsters that he has already slain.[50] Ninurta, using his
mystic mace, then launches a stormy assault against the demon, slays him, and takes away from him the stones of the
demon's army to build the world's first irrigation system. As
the text says:

"No one yet cleaned the little canals, the mud was not
dredged up. Ditch-making did not yet exist. People did not
work in furrows, barley was sown broadcast. [So] he made
a pile of stones in the Mountains. Like a floating cloud he
stretched out his arms over it. With a great wall, he barred
the front of the Land. He installed a sluice on the horizon.

The Hero acted cleverly, he dammed in the cities together. He blocked the powerful waters by means of stones. Now the waters will never again go down from the Mountains into the earth. That which was dispersed he gathered together. Where in the Mountains scattered lakes had formed, he joined them all together and led them down to the Tigris. He poured carp-floods of water over the fields."[51]

Ninurta then goes on to appoint the destinies of the different types of stones who marched against him: flint, for example, he curses, saying, "You were not equal to me who supported you. I shall rip you like a sack, and people will smash you into tiny pieces."[52] He then goes down the list, pronouncing the function and destiny of every stone used by the Sumerians, from alabaster and haematite to carnelian, lapis lazuli, diorite and gold, among many others.

Now, the alluvial plain, as I have mentioned, was poor in resources, especially in those of metals and minerals, almost all of which had to be imported from the mountain ranges to the north, east and west. Jane McIntosh summarizes the situation for us nicely in the following paragraph:

"Stone, used to make tools from the earliest times, served many purposes in Mesopotamia, although in the south, where stone was rare, tools were often made of wood or clay instead. Assyria had sandstone and limestone, and an outcrop of limestone at Ummayyad to the west of the lower Euphrates was probably exploited by the people of Babylonia. Assyria also had local supplies of alabaster in the upper Khabur region and flint along the Balikh and upper Euphrates. The Zagros foothills yielded lava, quartzite occurred in large amounts in the Hamrin, and gypsum was available in the Jebel Bishri. Some stone reached Babylonia as rocks carried down by the rivers: The quartzite, and perhaps the flint, used for tools at Tell 'Ouelli may have been transported in this way. Obsidian could be obtained from Anatolia, and basalt, diorite, granite, haematite, serpentine, and jasper were also imported from neighboring areas. Other decorative stones such as carnelian, steatite, agate, and lapis lazuli came from more distant Iranian, Afghan, or Indian sources."[53]

On another level, then, the story records the importation of metals and precious stones into Sumer from the various conquests—or else trade with—the peoples of the Zagros mountains and other areas rich in resources, like Anatolia and the Indus Valley. Asag and his army of stones, then, is both barbarian chieftain and yet also a personification of the mountainous source of the materials which the Sumerians transformed into "civilization." But I think the argument can be made that the Asag demon is, in addition, associated with the arts of the blacksmith and the craftsman, which Ninurta as a farmer god is specifically appropriating from him.

One clue that the Asag demon might also be a smith is that he is described as not only leading an army of stones—from whence the blacksmith will draw the metals from their ores—but that he is "deformed." All over the world, (as I remarked in this essay's Prologue) deformity is a trademark of the smith and the god of knowledge, whether we are considering the limp of Hephaestus, or Wieland's total inability to walk after he is hamstrung for offending the king, or Wotan's sacrificing of his eye at the Well of Knowledge to obtain the lore of the runes (and thus the medium of writing). Also, we must take note of the brief story recounting the Asag demon's origins, which states that Heaven copulated with the Earth goddess, who bore a warrior incapable of fear, knowing no father, "a murderer from the Mountains."[54] Asag's apparentage from the copulation of Heaven and Earth is very possibly a euphemism for a meteorite, from whence some metals, such as iron, were extracted by ancient smiths. The description of Asag as a warrior who knew no fear, furthermore, resembles that of Siegfried—of whom it was also said that he knew no fear—the warrior raised by the dwarf blacksmith Mimir, who taught him how to forge his own sword.

That Asag was a "murderer from the Mountains" is also consistent with the tradition that smiths are notoriously regarded as crafty, shifty and unreliable characters who are often portrayed as killers: think of the revenge of Wieland, for example, who carves up the king's children and makes trinkets out of their skulls and eyeballs; or of Daedalus, who was exiled from Athens because he had murdered his nephew Talos by pushing him from the top of a tower; or even Cain, the first murderer in Biblical history, whose son Tubal-cain became the first blacksmith (note that Cain's brother Abel, like Ninurta, was also a tiller of the soil, whereas Cain is elsewhere described as the inventor of the first cities).

In this story, then, we appear to have the oldest description of what will later become a cluster of attributes associated with the worldwide distribution of the smith archetype. This is, furthermore, the first time in the history of literature in which we are confronted with the archetype of the smith as a maker of mechanical monsters, for in this case, he sires an army of stone warriors from a mountain[55] (possibly a coded description of the activity of the smith: the ores that he digs out of the mountains are regarded as embryos which he will then transform into metals, as though he has "sired" them upon the mountains). Later, smiths like Hephaestus will make metal men. The smith Ilmarinen in *The Kalevala* makes a metal woman so cold and unappealing that

69

Vainamoinen cannot bear to lie with her.[56] There is also an African Zulu myth which features a "deformed" child who becomes a smith and creates an army of metal men. The tale is recounted by William Leiss as follows:

"In accordance with the prevailing customs a woman brought her newborn baby to the two-headed talking birds who bestowed names on all children. This child was hideously deformed and the birds, discerning the presence of terrible evil in it, announced in alarm that the child would have to be destroyed at once. The mother rebelled against the judgment and escaped into the jungle, where she remained hiding in a deep cave, raising her child in the bowels of the earth.

One day the mother noticed that under the young boy's fixed gaze iron ore began to melt. Out of the ore he fashioned a flying metal robot with powerful teeth and jaws, and when his mother begged him to destroy his creation he instead ordered the robot to kill her. Then he created an army of similar robots and, emerging from the cave, led his forces against the two-headed birds, utterly destroying them and conquering the world.

He established himself as supreme ruler, and all the world's people lived in perfect comfort, since the innumerable mechanical creatures acted as their slaves and performed every task. Gradually men and women lost their ability to do anything at all, even reproduce their kind. So the robots created semi-human zombies out of animal flesh which were capable of reproduction.

The Tree of Life and the earth goddess were appalled at this interference with their sacred functions, however, and resolved to destroy the offenders. They sent a huge flood, but the ruler ordered the robots to build gigantic rafts upon which the many survivors could live permanently, while he and his court reveled in even greater luxury than before. Since the sun was continually hidden by storm clouds, the ruler directed the construction of an artificial one, which in the people's opinion shone more brilliantly than had the real sun. But finally the goddess and the Tree of Life marshaled overwhelming forces and obliterated all traces of this evil civilization." [57]

This myth is very similar to the Ninurta tale and demonstrates the world-wide fear and resistance to technological innovations that have a culturally disintegrative effect on many societies. Such societies are conservative for a reason—for they fear the smith and his uncanny powers—so the blacksmith as a character is rarely featured in a positive light in ancient myths.

So if the Asag demon is the first smith to appear in recorded literature, it would appear that by the time of King Gudea of Lagash (c. 2141 BC) technology was already being viewed with a certain skepticism, especially by the more conservative farmer.

It is not surprising that the farmer might have come to regard the smith as a threat not only to his way of life, but as a danger to society as a whole, for the smith is an itinerant wanderer who always hires himself out to the highest bidder, for whom he then makes the very weapons that the barbarians from the mountains use to attack the cities. And of course, when a city-state is attacked by marauding nomads, typically the first people to suffer are the farmers working their fields out on the peripheries.

Enki vs. Enlil

There is a line which occurs near the end of the Ninurta story in which the gods are giving praise to him after his victory, a line which reads: "Hero, deluge without equal, the *enki* and *ninki* deities do not dare to resist you."[58] Now I am not an Assyriologist, but the phrase "*enki* and *ninki* deities" sounds to me an awful lot like the *enkum* and *ninkum*, who were priests in the temple of the god Enki at Mesopotamia's southernmost city of Eridu (and also one of its most ancient, going clear back to 6,000 BC). The *enkum* and *ninkum* were, in addition, creatures associated with his watery abyss, the *abzu*, whom he sent hunting in pursuit of Inanna after she got Enki drunk and stole the tablets of the *me*'s from him. Either way, they are associated with the cult of Enki, which is, according to this line in the story, explicitly subordinated to the might of Ninurta.

What is interesting about this fact is that Enki was known as the patron god of smiths and craftsmen. He was the Sumerian god of intelligence *par excellence*, and also of the making of any form or shape. Indeed, one of his epithets is *Nudimmud*, which means "image maker." And it is indeed the case that when we survey a number of other Sumerian myths, we find a consistent tradition of conflict between Enki, the patron god of smiths and craftsmen, and Ninurta, the god of farmers.

Most of the battles are by proxy, however, with the exception of the tale known as "Ninurta and the Turtle." It is only a fragment from a much larger story that seems to be related to the cycle in which Ninurta slays the Anzu bird for its theft of the tablets of the *me*'s, for as the fragment begins, the conflict is just winding down. (The *me*'s, incidentally, are the "software" without which civilization cannot run).

Ninurta has freed the tablets from the Anzu bird and returned them to the *abzu*, where Enki is in charge of them. But Ninurta now believes that he deserves them for himself, so he enters the palace of the *abzu* with the intention of taking them back. However, Enki always foreknows what is going to happen (like Prometheus, god of "forethought")—for he is the god of the mind, corresponding in the Sumerian pantheon to Hermes-Mercury in the classical world—and so he fashions a turtle made out of clay which digs a pit near the gate of the *abzu*. When Ninurta steps near it, the turtle reaches out and grabs his ankle, pulling him down into the hole with him. Then, as the text reads, Enki said to him: "...you who set your mind to kill me...who makes big claims, I cut down, I raise up. You who set your sights on me like this—what has your position seized for you now? Where has your strength fled? Where is your heroism? In the great mountains, you caused destruction, but how will you get out now?"[59]

Hence, the story clearly records a tradition of conflict between Ninurta and Enki—and the conflict may actually have been about that of the two priesthoods of Nippur and Eridu vying for supremacy. But there are other tales in which the collision between the two gods can only be intuited, as in the famous story of "The Tale of Adapa," in which Enki has fashioned the first man, a being named Adapa—who will later become one of the seven *apkallu*, or sages, who will transform into fish in order to survive the Great Flood so that they may teach the arts of civilization to the remnants of humanity. (One of Adapa's epithets is "Uan," which appears to be a pun on the word for "craftsman.")[60]

Adapa goes out every day in his little boat to supply the temple of his god Enki—most likely at Eridu—with fish, for Enki is a god who is traditionally linked with fish. But one day while out on the marsh, the South Wind comes up and causes a storm, overturning his boat. As a result, Adapa curses the South Wind, which has the magical effect of breaking its wing so that the wind does not blow for seven days. The high god Anu finds out about this, becomes furious and decides to summon Adapa to his court in heaven. Enki, foreknowing all, warns him, telling him that he will be offered the bread and water of death but that he must refuse to take it. However, Adapa is advised to disguise himself as a mourner, and when the two gods at the threshold to heaven greet him, Dumuzi and Ningishzidda, and inquire for whom he is mourning, he tells them that two gods have disappeared from the land and he is mourning for them, namely, Dumuzi and Ningishzidda. Flattered, the pair decides to put in a good word for Adapa with Anu, who presently summons the human before him. When Adapa explains what has happened, Anu chooses instead to reward him and offer the bread and water not of death but of immortal life: Adapa, however, following Enki's advice, refuses them, and in doing so, loses the chance to bring immortality into the world. Instead, he actually brings death, plague and disease back down to earth with him, although Anu institutes a special decree for the goddess (probably Gula, wife of Ninurta) to cure all such ills.[61]

On the surface, this story would appear to have nothing to do with Ninurta, until we note two salient facts, one of which is pointed out by George Roux: "It so happens," he says, "that the south (-easterly) wind is of capital importance to agriculture in southern Iraq, for it brings what little rain there is in winter, and in summer causes the ripening of the dates…"[62]

Thus, Dumuzi, the god associated with the date palm, has apparently been killed by Adapa's act (which is why, according to Roux, Adapa finds him in heaven) due to the failure of the South Wind to blow, and so Adapa's killing of this wind has caused severe damage to the crops. The second point, however, is that the South Wind, as we learn from Samuel Noah Kramer, was associated specifically with the god Ninurta, the patron god of farmers.[63] So Enki, by proxy through his servant craftsman Adapa, has struck yet another blow at Ninurta and the farmers.

Notice, too, how this story evinces the farmer's mistrust of the craftsman gods of the city and their specifically civic, rather than rural, interests, for plague, death and illness— in the form of both crop failure and human mortality—are seen to have been brought into the world by Adapa, a being associated specifically with technology and craftsmanship, just as Cain, whose name means "smith," brings the first murder into the world. Thus, the story evidences a certain skepticism of blindly putting one's faith in the gods of technology. They are the ones, the story seems to imply,who are always meddling with the secret forces of nature in ways that are dangerous to human civilization.

Ninurta, furthermore, was the son of the farmer god Enlil, the inventor of the hoe. Enlil, too, was a storm god who was pictured as living on top of a mountain. There is also a long tradition of conflict between Enlil and Enki, the two great gods of ancient Sumer after the high god An. Taken together, these three gods were associated with the four temporal compass points, since they are linked with what are known as the Three Ways: the Way of Enlil, which corresponds to the Tropic of Cancer; the Way of Enki to the Tropic of Capricorn; while the two equinoxes, associated with due East, correspond to the Way of Anu, their father.[64]

According to all variations of the flood myth, furthermore, Enlil is always the god who decides to wipe humanity out with the flood because they are too noisy and he cannot get enough sleep. But Enki persistently defies him and chooses to save *one* human being—variously named Ziusudra, Atrahasis or Utnapishtim—in order to instruct him about the secrets for building an ark within which the plans for reconstructing civilization after the floodwaters recede will be kept safe.

So, in Sumerian myth, civilization and the destiny of humanity are caught between the struggles of a farmer god and a smith / craftsman god. Note, too, that Enlil, the god of farmers like his son Ninurta, ultimately cares nothing for civilization and is willing to wipe it out, utterly, just as Zeus does in Greek myth. It is the craftsman god Enki who is careful about preparing a floating monastery that will make provisions for the survival of civilization through the coming Dark Age.

Clearly, then, the Mesopotamians were ambivalent about technology. On the one hand, they regarded it as the most important thing in the world, since Enki, unlike the deities of many other traditions, is a craftsman god who is one of the three highest and most honored gods of the civilization. Smith and craftsmen gods in other societies generally do not hold such honor. When we note the high gods of the Hindus: Shiva, Vishnu, Brahma and Devi; or the Greeks: Zeus, Poseidon and Hades; we note the conspicuous absence of a technology god at the top of the pantheon. In Greece, Hermes is a god of the mind and writing, and he is one of the highest gods of the pantheon, but he is not a smith. He is a maker, at best, of lyres, but not weapons, trinkets and implements. That function is handled by Hephaestus (Roman Vulcan) whom, take note, was a god given very little respect by the other Olympians. He was reviled, abused, kicked out of heaven and cuckolded. (He was furthermore, given the odious task of chaining Prometheus—the god who originally brought technology to humanity—to a rock at the top of a mountain).

It is only in Mesopotamia that one of the three most revered gods is associated with technology and this tells us something about how highly the Sumerians valued it (after all, they invented civilization as we have come to know it: writing, astronomy, mathematics, etc.) But at the same time, as their various flood and catastrophe myths show us, they knew that technology was a potentially destructive force that could lead to social unrest, change and destabilization; salinization of the soil, silting up of the canals, overcrowding of the cities, wars, plague and disease, all these things in Mesopotamian myth are linked with technology as their root cause. So this was a civilization that was ambivalent, to say the least, about this "gift" from the gods that it bequeathed to the human race.

(2005)

The Dawning of the Metaphysical Age

A Few Words About the Cover Painting:

Prometheus Being Chained by Vulcan

The work of art on this book's cover, *Prometheus Being Chained by Vulcan* was painted in 1623 by an artist of the Dutch Utrecht School named Dirck van Baburen. The artists of this school modeled their work after that of Caravaggio, and the present painting in particular bears the obvious influence of Caravaggio's 1601 *Crucifixion of St. Peter*, for in both paintings, the protagonists are being crucified in upside down positions.

But the myth that van Baburen is referring to in his painting comes from the opening scene of Aeschylus's *Prometheus Bound*, when the blacksmith god Hephaestus (Roman Vulcan) has been ordered by Zeus to chain Prometheus to a rock on the edge of a mountain (though Aeschylus does not specify that it is the Caucasus).[65] In van Baburen's painting, it looks as though he has displaced the scene from a mountain to the interior of Vulcan's smithy, for it is a cavern-

81

ous room that glows with lava-like fire in the background.

Prometheus—who is not mentioned in Homer, but first appears in Hesiod (although both authors make references to Hephaestus)—is being punished for his famous act of stealing fire from the heavens and bringing it down to humanity, a race of mortals which, in later traditions of the fourth century BC, Prometheus was regarded as having created out of clay. But he has a particular fondness for mortals and always favors them throughout all the traditions: in Hesiod's account, Prometheus tricked Zeus by wrapping the meat of a slain ox in a hide and in another hide the bones of the ox cleverly dipped in fat and asked Zeus to choose the better sacrificial offering. Zeus, easily deceived, chose the portion containing only the bones and fat, thus setting the precedent for all future sacrificial offerings to the gods, giving them only the bones, while mortals got the benefit of the meat.[66] Zeus, however, in his anger, hid fire so that humans would not be able to use it to cook their meat. But Prometheus then stole the fire from the heavens and wrapped it in a fennel-stalk and brought it down to men so that they could cook their food.

Zeus's response, according to Hesiod, was to order Hephaestus to create the woman Pandora out of clay, who was then responsible for bringing all evils into the world. Then he chained Prometheus on a pillar—although Hesiod does not mention Hephaestus doing this but rather Zeus—[67]where he was bound to stay in agony while every day an eagle came and ate his liver, which grew back again each day (the eagle can be glimpsed in the upper left corner of van Baburen's painting). Only Heracles would come one day to shoot the eagle with his arrows and liberate Prometheus from his sufferings.

Aeschylus, however, has Prometheus not only stealing

fire but teaching human beings *all* the arts of civilization. Prometheus narrates his story from his crag to the Chorus, explaining that before he came along, men lived in caves and knew nothing of tilling the soil, or astronomy or mathematics or medicine until he taught it to them.[68] But it was the theft of fire that sealed his fate, and so Aeschylus has the blacksmith god chain him to the mountainside.

In some traditions, it was Hermes who did this, but Hermes puts in an appearance near the end of *Prometheus Bound* on behalf of Zeus demanding that Prometheus tell him the secret that his mother Themis confided in him about the son of Zeus that would one day overthrow his rule. This is perhaps why van Baburen has Hermes standing in the background of his painting, bemused by the sufferings of Prometheus, but in Aeschylus's play, Prometheus has nothing but scorn for Hermes and regards him condescendingly as merely Zeus's errand boy. He refuses to give up the secret, a secret which would undoubtedly have been revealed in the now lost remaining plays of the trilogy.

Prometheus—whose name, of course, means "forethought"—is a Titan who has a certain affection for mortal humans, while Zeus scorns them: indeed, in the myth of the Four World Ages that Hesiod recounts in his *Works and Days*, Zeus wipes them out of existence on more than one occasion.[69] Indeed, the enmity between Prometheus and Zeus reminds one of that between Enki and Enlil in ancient Sumerian myth, for Enki was the god of craftsmen, too, and was always looking out for the well-being of human mortals. The fact that he saved them from complete destruction by the flood sent upon them by Enlil—also, like Zeus, a thunder god—through instructing the flood hero Utnapishtim how to build an ark, finds its parallel in Greek myth in the fact that the son of Prometheus was Deucalion, the Greek

83

flood hero, whom he instructed to regenerate the human race by casting stones over his shoulder.

Thus, Prometheus—the god of technology—and his consistent antagonisms with Zeus, the rustic thunder god on high, is a dyad that structurally repeats the earlier one between Enki, the patron of craftsmen, and Enlil (together with his son Ninurta) the rustic farmer gods. In the post-metaphysical age, when the gods have fled (Holderlin) and become mere signifiers, a similar opposition between the rustic philosopher Heidegger dwelling in his cabin in the Black Forest and writing treatises against the globalizing world of empty consumerism unfolding all about him will be a much later echo of these same conflicts.[70] Ted Kaczynski, too, building bombs in *his* rustic cabin in the woods to be hurled at scientists in order to put a stop to Industrial Society will replay the myth of Ninurta against the Asag demon, or Enlil against Enki in modern guise on the plane of the Real rather than the Imaginary of gods, myths and rituals. But the structure of the antagonism will remain the same across the millenia.

Hesiod's *Theogony* culminates with Zeus's war against the Titans, which brings the Golden Age of the rule of his father Kronos and his Titan brothers to an end. Zeus then thrusts the Titans down into Tartaros, the Underworld, while Prometheus is chained—although not for siding with the Titans, but rather with humans—and his brother Atlas is consigned to forever bear the globe of the cosmos upon his shoulders. Typhon is overthrown and cast down beneath Mount Aetna, at the top of which, in Aeschylus's play, Hephaestus sets up his forge.

Zeus, the god of transcendence—for he is a sky god—then gives birth to Athena from the metaphysical vulva that he has now interiorized into his skull, while Hera (according to Hesiod) then gives birth parthenogenetically to Hephaestus in response.[71] (Hera, however, repulsed by the smith's deformed features, simply tosses him out of Olympus, where he goes plunging like a meteorite into the earth's oceans). Athena is the goddess of reason and her temple is built atop the Acropolis in Athens as the metaphysical age—with its logocentrism—is about to begin.

In van Baburen's painting, the presence of Hermes in the background suggests that as the pre-metaphysical age is drawing to its close—with the casting down of the Titans, the various monsters and serpentine deities of the age of myth and mysticism—writing is now looming on the horizon, for Hermes was the god of communication. As Vilem Flusser pointed out, writing emerged amongst the Greeks and the Jews as a criticism of myths and images: whereas myths run round in circles, writing unrolls the circles into one-dimensional lines of text that undo the myths precisely through criticizing them. Every writer, as he puts it, is a demythologizer.[72]

And so, with the birth of Athena as goddess of rationality, and with logocentric Zeus ruling from on high, while his messenger Hermes stands at his side, the metaphysical age begins to dawn. Whenever the gods of a previous age, such as the Titans, are scrapped by tossing them down into an Underworld, you know that an old environment is being dismantled by the advent of new media that are coming into being as vehicles through which the new structure of consciousness—in this case, Jean Gebser's mental structure—conveys itself. Milton in his *Paradise Lost* scraps all the gods of antiquity by tossing them into *his* Underworld.[73]

And there is not much of a leap from the ascendance of the Olympians to the Forms of Plato: both are transcendent, and both have a sense of metaphysical certitude about them that cannot be brooked. Heidegger marked the official start of the metaphysical age with Plato's divorce of Being from Becoming, but remember, too, that Plato was not fond of the arts. Plato, like Ninurta, Enlil and Zeus before him, had strong ties to the countryside and no faith in artists and poets whatsoever. His aesthetic theory that the artist is only capable of producing a work that merely copies the realm of appearances, itself already a copy or dim reflection of the numinously glowing transcendent Forms,[74] bears not a little of Zeus's and Enlil's mistrust of the gods of the craftsman, of technology and of the city. The work of art, for Plato, is thrice removed from Being, and so he bans poets from his ideal state.

Beginning with the Renaissance, in which mathematically correct principles were used to fathom the art of depth perspective in painting—thus bringing art closer to science—art and science have gradually become ever more and more closely wed together until with photography, the cinema and radio, they are scarcely distinguishable. Indeed, nowadays, art almost cannot be done without the use of hi-tech equipment like computers, cameras and video-imaging machines of all kinds.

Today's artist in the post-metaphysical age is also a technologist, and it is almost certain that gods like Ninurta or Enlil, or philosophers such as Plato would have condemned them for allowing technology to gain the upper hand over art. Certainly Heidegger did, as is well known and documented in his essays.

So Prometheus would not stay bound for long, but the very machines that he would let loose upon the world would slowly and gradually tear apart the Transcendental Signifieds and Iconotypes of God, Crucifixion and Apocalypse, leaving behind only a realm of floating signifiers—billboards, ads, celebrities—drifting like ice floes across an uncertain ontological surface with no place to anchor them.

And that is the situation, today, that we now find ourselves in.

There is no firm firmament with permanent constellations above our heads anchoring meaning in metaphysical certitude.

For they have all been drowned out by the incandescence of the glowing lights of our sprawling cities.

(2016)

The Post-Metaphysical Age

From the Myth of Tammuz to the

Collapse of the Signifieds:

A Look at Paul Bowles's Novel

The Sheltering Sky

Collapsed Macrospheres

The Sheltering Sky was the first novel published by the American expatriate writer Paul Bowles in 1949, and it tells the story of an American couple named Port and Kit Moresby, who are, as Port insists, "travelers" (rather than tourists, who are always anxious to get back home) on their way from New York City to a journey across the desert terrains of North Africa. It is specifically the West from which they are trying to escape, moving always ever further eastward. Port, it seems, is a man with no occupation, although his passport indicates that he is a "writer"—one, be it said, who has never written anything. But he is fascinated with maps, for his mind is always on the next unexplored horizon, much to his wife Kit's annoyance. The couple, who have been married for twelve years, are traveling with a man named Tunner, a mutual friend, and as the novel opens, they have just arrived in a North African coastal city—perhaps Algiers—with the intent of gradually moving south and east into the vast reaches of the Sahara Desert.

The story is a simple one told in three parts: in Book One, "Tea in the Sahara," the trio encounter another pair of (in this case, unpleasant) travelers known as the Lyles, an overbearing mother and her son who is always asking Port for money. In this section, the Moresbys and Tunner travel gradually south, from Algiers to Boussif—and then eastward—from Boussif to Ain Krorfa, the landscape becoming more and more dilapidated and inhospitable to the comfort expectations of the Westerner, especially Tunner, who is forever complaining of the lack of decent accommodations.

In Book Two, "The Earth's Sharp Edge," the Moresbys have separated from Tunner (whom they have palmed off on the Lyles), their travelling companion increasingly disliked by Port, who rightly senses Tunner's growing interest in his wife Kit. But then Port becomes ill as they are traveling by bus from Ain Krorfa to Bou Noura, and Kit grows alarmed at her husband's rapid descent into an unspecified illness that renders him incapable of even standing upright. Soon, she is dragging him from one town to the next in search of adequate medical treatment, but it is in the town of Sba, located somewhere in the deep deserts of the Sahara, where Port dies of the illness, leaving Kit alone, and with Tunner on the prowl after her. She hides from him after the death of her husband, and spends the night alone under a tamarisk tree.

In Book Three, "The Sky," Kit is picked up by a camel

caravan which is led by an Arab named Belqassim, who immediately treats her as his acquired property. The caravan follows the smooth dune-shaped spaces of the deep desert where Belqassim takes his new wife, the American Kit Moresby, to his own flat-roofed mud-brown house in a village somewhere in the Soudan. He already has three wives, but he has disguised Kit with a burnous to resemble a man, and locks her away in a separate mud-brick apartment from the rest of his compound. But the wives, who are jealous of the time he spends with her, soon pry their way in when Belqassim is gone on an outing and strip Kit of her clothing, confirming that she is indeed a woman. Out of jealousy, they allow Kit to escape one day—she also bribes them with her jewelry—and she is found wandering in the desert by the local authorities who turn her over to the French government. Kit's mind, by this point, is gone, and she is flown north across the desert back to Algiers as a sort of psych-ward patient with which no one knows what to do. While waiting in the taxi cab parked in front of a hotel for her proprietress, Kit escapes once again, and at the end of the novel, she has disappeared into the city streets of Algiers near the very same café, the Café d'Eckmuhl-Noiseux, where the narrative had begun, thus coming back full circle to the very spot of the novel's inception.

The key to the novel's title comes when, in Book One, Kit and Port are out bicycling in the desert one day. They have climbed up to the top of a ridge that gives them an excellent view out over the desert, and Port tells Kit that he often has the feeling that the sky is a solid thing, "protecting us," as he puts it, "from what's behind." When Kit inquires about what it's protecting them from, he says, "Nothing, I suppose. Just darkness. Absolute night." His response terrifies Kit, and rightfully so, since the novel itself is a fathoming of its ontological consequences. In other words, the dome of the "sheltering sky" is a classic Sloterdijkian macrosphere:[75] it is composed of a tissue of myths, cosmologies, ontologies and transcendental signifieds that provide an entire civilization with its metaphysical immune system. It creates, and sustains, the realm of what theoretician Boris Groys—in his book *On the New*—calls "cultural values."[76] Outside, and beyond such a cultural macrosphere, lies the "profane world" of the value systems of other cultures.

Kit and Port, then, in migrating from their American cosmopolis of New York City, have moved out into the profane world that exists beyond the pale of their own civilization. They are no longer protected from the abyss of nihilism that civilizational macrospheres are meant to immunize the individual against, and so they are prey to its impacts. And indeed, the impacts of an alien culture, in this novel, turn out to be absolutely devastating. It is as though a Roman citizen living in the days of the empire had crossed the liminal boundaries of the ecumene—the Rhine River, let's say—and ventured out into the remote wildernesses of the tribal world of Scandinavia or Saxony, totally unprepared for the encounter with alien cultural values.

The novel, then, does *not* perpetuate Edward Said's famous critique of what he terms Western "Orientalism,"[77] which began in the West at about the time of Napoleon's entry into Egypt (or perhaps slightly before), and which spawned the generation of Orientalist painters from Delacroix's *Women of Algiers* in 1814 to Ingres's *Turkish Bath* of 1862. Indeed, the novel opens with just such an image as, one night in Algiers when Port is bored, he goes for a walk and is led into a bordello by a man who takes him down a long flight of steps to a series of tents where he encounters a prostitute named Marhnia, whom Bowles describes with a dreamy, seductive mystique about her that is straight out of an Orientalist painting. (Indeed, she may as well be Ingres's *Odalisque*). But, as Said insists, from the Orientalist point of view, the East is always portrayed as dreamy, mystical and under-developed, and the West somehow is always seen as rational, progressive and modern. It is, of course, a viewpoint anchored in the West's metaphysical age—a term constructed by Heidegger—an age which is structured by what Derrida has termed "transcendental signifieds,"[78] or ultimate metaphysical categories such as God, freedom or the soul which anchor a privileged (Western) point of view from which all other metaphysical systems are regarded, and dismissed, as "Other" (and hence, inferior).

But Bowles, as a post-World War II expatriate American who spent his life living and writing in North Africa, is not perpetuating the clichés of Orientalism at all, but rather *undoing* and *dismantling* their codes. *The Sheltering Sky* as an image refers to the Western metaphysical macrosphere, but it was precisely this macrosphere built out of transcendental signifieds (which I have written about in my book *Art After Metaphysics*)[79] that collapsed during and immediately after World War II. The art of Mark Rothko, for instance, with its shift from Modernist iconotypes to postmodern nihilism, provides us with a visual chronicle of this collapse as he moves into the discovery of his "multiforms," which are liquefying shapes of collapsed Modernist iconotypes, and then onward into his universe of squares of glowing, luminous light (which I have termed "elementary units of Being").[80] But in Rothko's later work, he moved on to uncover and indeed, to "unconceal" what Heidegger termed in his essay "What is Metaphysics?" "the Nothing,"[81] especially with the sheer black canvases of the de Menil Chapel (1964).

In a way, then, Bowles is Rothko's literary analogue: a

fellow New Yorker—Bowles spent his life growing up in and around New York—who became disillusioned with Modernism and traded it out for the interesting and more, as he felt, culturally authentic world of North African civilization. Thus, the "absolute darkness" that Port speaks of, which lies *behind* the sheltering sky, is an almost exact analogue to Rothko's "Nothing" that he discovers, in his all-black canvases, lying behind and beyond his "elementary units of Being." *No* points of view, whatsoever, in this age, i.e. the post-metaphysical age—which has endured up to the present day—can be privileged any longer as metaphysically superior to any other.[82] The West's own sheltering sky, with its tissue of cosmologies composed out of a cellular matrix of transcendent Ideas, is now *gone*. Bowles's novel is therefore titled ironically, for it is precisely the *absence* of a protective macrosphere that imperils his protagonists (things are done *to* them; they themselves never *do* anything). Bowles, and indeed, with the three other novels which he wrote after *The Sheltering Sky*—*Let it Come Down* (1952), *The Spider's House* (1955) and *Up Above the World* (1966)—was chronicling the devastating metaphysical consequences that ensue when one's own civilizational macrosphere is no longer functioning to protect one against the impacts of the Real.

Sign Regimes

It is all a matter, as Deleuze and Guattari have shown us, of codes and coding.[83] A particular sign regime (which corresponds, more or less, to Peter Sloterdijk's concept of a macrosphere) is a sign system composed of signifiers that overcode other, usually older, sign regimes. As they put it in *A Thousand Plateaus*, no sign regime is pure. They are always mixed, since cultural hybridization is the norm, not the exception.[84]

As Port and Kit move east, therefore, they move *away* from the Western metaphysical sign regime—the very sign regime of metaphysical self-certainties that had created the colonialization process, and hence gave rise to Said's Orientalist attitude of superiority and condescension toward the East in the first place—and toward the sign regime of an alien culture (or if you prefer, what Boris Groys terms "the profane realm" of the value systems that exist *outside* those of one's own culture, or realm of "cultural values").[85] As they move about through the wilderness of the Saharan Desert, they are indeed no longer protected by "the sheltering" sign regime of the West, but are immunologically prey to impacts from the profane realm of a cultural world which they do not understand at all, but have, at the outset, dreamily imagined in the typical Orientalist fashion as a realm of escape into a perpetual hypnotic trance of hashish and alluring bordello / harem women. But, as it turns out, the alien world which they discover has its own laws and its own sign regime with unique codes, and the further they move away from the geographical (and hence semiological) landscape of Western civilization, the more they are slowly overcoded by the alien sign regime of Islamic North Africa (itself a westward migration from the Middle East). There is no room for condescension here, only terror and the anxiety of disorientation as Port and Kit are swallowed up by another sign regime altogether. The West, in *The Sheltering Sky*, does *not* come out on top, but is completely dismantled and gobbled up by Eastern codes.

This process of semiological overcoding is not a new one. Indeed, in reading Gibbon's *Decline and Fall of the Roman Empire*—a classic Orientalist treatise of condescension

97

and patronization toward the East if ever there was one—the reader can nevertheless, despite Gibbon's Western metaphysical age bias, make out the lineaments of an earlier version of the same process, for he portrays the decline of the Roman Empire as a gradual *darkening* of the West and a *lighting up* of the East. In Heideggerian terms, that is, during the period from about 200 AD onward, the Western Clearing of Being began to grow dark and to withdraw into concealment, while the Clearing itself began, simultaneously, to light up in the East and to stay lit until about the 15th or 16th centuries, when the reverse process began to occur: the West has been lit up ever since, while the East has lapsed into darkness (and I say this as an historical observation—since everything bearing the stamp of novelty and "the new" in the world today has originated in Europe since then; I do *not* say this as a way of denigrating the East).

With Gibbon, however, one must pay attention to the details: the Roman Empire, as his narrative evolves, is actually composed of *two* civilizations, a Western Roman Empire—centered at Rome and Ravenna—and an Eastern Roman Empire whose core lay in Byzantium. The two languages of the ecumene, from about the second century AD onward, were Latin and Greek: Latin for the West and Greek for the Byzantine world. The Gospels, as is well known, were written in Greek, though their words were spoken in Aramaic by its protagonists, an apparently innocuous detail until we note that Marcus Aurelius Antoninus wrote his *Meditations*, not in Latin, but in Greek at around 180 AD. And as the Age of the Antonines is the Golden Age of the Five Emperors—Nerva, Trajan, Hadrian and the two Antonines—with which Gibbon begins his narrative, followed by the inception of its decline (or darkening, as Heidegger might say) with the debauched emperor Commodus (hence, Joyce's 98 "commodious vicus of recirculation"), the detail becomes glaringly significant as the beginnings of an overcoding process of the Eastern sign regime *over* that of the West. The ascension of Elagabalus to the throne in 218 continues the process, since, as Gibbon puts it disparagingly, Elagabalus was the first Asiatic ruler of the empire, as he was born and raised in Syria.[86] With the sacking of Rome in 410 AD, then, the light goes out of the West altogether and the balance tilts toward Byzantium as the sole inheritor of the sign regime of antiquity, with Greek as its official language. The rise of the Persian Sassanians in the East, from about 200 to 650 AD, with its restoration—or, perhaps "unconcealment"—of the Achaemenid Dynasty (overcoded and gobbled up by the Greeks under Alexander), indicates the shifting of the center of gravity of the Clearing of civilization toward the East and of the overcoding of the West by Eastern signifiers. Even the story of Islam, from the Ummayads centered at Damascus in its first century or so to the construction of Baghdad around 762 AD as the axial center of the Abbasid Caliphate which succeeded it,[87] continues the story of this Eastward drift of the Clearing.

The West did not light up again until perhaps the 15th century, the time of the Renaissance, which took place simultaneously with the swallowing up of the Byzantine Civilization by the Ottomans, themselves representing a stiffening and petrifaction of the Islamic civilization which began to set in from about that time. Today, if one may say so without being accused of Orientalist bias, it is the West which has lit up and become the primary Clearing for Civilization (for it has defined the ontological status of the "new"), while the East has lapsed into a state of reactionary "darkening." Hence, the journey of Port and Kit beyond the pale of New York City would be analogous to that of a Roman citizen crossing the Rhine River in the time of the Empire. That is to say, it is an entry into "darkening" and into a realm of the culturally "profane" (which, be it said, is always relative to one's own civilizational standpoint) beyond the codes of one's own native sign regime.

By a process that is analogous to the overcoding of the West by Eastern signifiers from about 200 AD onward, as Port and Kit move further east in the narrative of *The Sheltering Sky* and deeper into the Sahara Desert, they are slowly overcoded by Eastern signifiers. Beginning in Chapter 15—the exact middle of the book going by number of chapters since, like a complete moon cycle, there are exactly 30 chapters—the first Eastern signifiers start to appear and slowly engulf the narrative as a swarm of flies appears on the bus in which Port and Kit are traveling to Ain Krorfa (where Port first begins to sicken with an internal sense of being cold all the time). The flies, straight out of the Book of Exodus, indicate the novel's first appearance of a "waste land" motif, a motif that had its beginnings in Near Eastern mythology in Mesopotamia in which, with the death of the god Tammuz, all of nature dried up and began to weep for the passing of the dead god. The Waste Land motif emerges here and, like a black creeper vine, grows ever larger as the narrative progresses.[88]

Indeed, it is precisely the Near Eastern myth of the dying and reviving god (and most especially that of Tammuz) that Port is plugged into. Lacking the immunization of his own cultural macrosphere, Port is recoded by Eastern myth. His death is a modern performance of the myth of the Babylonian god Tammuz, who dies in the summer (the Arabs named the month of July after him) when the heat of the desert dries out all the plants, and is revived again in the autumn, when Ishtar descends into the underworld to bring him back, and along with him, all the crops. One need only think of the fate of Gilgamesh's companion Enkidu in the Babylonian *Gilgamesh Epic*, who also dies of a slow, wasting sickness and is specifically and consciously plugged into the role of Tammuz by the epic's author (who describes all of Uruk weeping for Enkidu, just like Tammuz), for the signifiers to become clear.[89]

With respect to the fate of Kit, then, the Eastern recoding process continues to unfold, for her story in Book Three is overlaid by the myth of the abduction of the maiden into the underworld by King Death, which is one of the East's (both Near and Far) main myth motifs. It appears in Greek myth, too (i.e. Persephone; Cupid and Psyche, etc.), but its most charismatic examples are found in the East: the very plot of the *Ramayana*, for instance, hinges on the abduction of Sita by Ravana to the underworld domain of Sri Lanka; or the abduction of the goddess Earth by the elephant demon in the *Puranas*, while Vishnu in his boar avatar must descend to the bottom of the ocean to fetch her back. Indeed, the most evident comparison—to my mind—comes to us from the *Eighteen Songs of a Nomad Flute* composed by Liu Shang during the Tang Dynasty (618-907 AD) and later illustrated under the Emperor Gaozong of the Song Dynasty in the twelfth century.[90] In that tale, Xiongnu barbarians enter the Chinese capital of Chang'an and sack the city, taking as their hostage the poetess and composer Cai Wenji. The narrative then describes her unhappiness living as a captive to the barbarians of the steppe, and wistfully yearning for her homeland, to which she is returned by way of a ransom, twelve years later. (Kit and Port, incidentally, have been married exactly twelve years, one complete revolution of the planet Jupiter around the sun).

Thus, as the narrative of *The Sheltering Sky* proceeds, it is gradually overcoded by an Eastern sign regime that dis-

101

solves, liquefies and dismantles all Western metaphysical structures. The "sheltering sky" that would have protected Kit and Port has indeed collapsed, rendering them prey to reterritorialization by a culture which they cannot, and do not, understand.

Blue Dome

There is one further point to make about the overcoding process of *The Sheltering Sky*: that of the blue dome. The blue dome is also part of the Eastern sign regime in a way that is not the case in the West, which dismantled what Oswald Spengler called the cavern cosmology of the Magian civilization first evident in the art of Giotto, who begins to substitute the gold background of the Byzantine cavern with the blue sky, indicating an opening up and expanse of space as the dome of the East is shattered by the Western sign regime with its sublime taste for the expanses of Infinite Space.[91] In the Western sign regime, the color blue becomes associated with the infinity of the daytime sky and is borne by the robes of Mary as such, but in the East, blue was painted on the *outside* of the domes of their mosques and churches, while the interior was often colored gold and covered with geometric arabesques indicative of a shutting off and closing down of the infinitudes of space.

The Dome of the Rock, built under the Umayyad caliph Abd-al-Malik (685-705 AD), is the first great mosque of Islam, and it was constructed in Jerusalem around 690 AD specifically as a rival to the Ka'aba in Mecca.[92] At the time, an anti-Caliph named Abdallah ibn-Zubair had taken control of Mecca, claiming the right of descent through Mohammed's favorite wife Aisha, and after he was overthrown by Malik around 692, the Dome of the Rock was built over the rock upon which Abraham had supposedly attempted to sacrifice his son Isaac.[93] That rock, then, was meant to rival the Black Stone at Mecca, and it was covered by an octagonal structure with a blue dome on the outside: a sheltering sky, in other words, to enclose Abraham's rock inside of a cavern. When the city of Baghdad was built in 762 AD, it too had a mosque with a blue dome that was built in the center of the city, although as Islamic mosque architecture migrates across North Africa, it was the minaret rather than the dome that became the favored and more pronounced structure.[94] The dome, as in the Shiraz mosques of Persia, became more emphasized in Eastern Islam than in Western.

Nonetheless, the sheltering sky of the protective macrosphere of the West's metaphysical age—compare with Jean Gebser's Integral Sphere that he sees capturing the entirety of Modernist Art within it—is, in Bowles's novel *missing* precisely because it has collapsed, together with all the transcendental signifieds ornamented, as it were, across its surface and which had anchored all metaphysical self-certainties in the West, and it is traded out for the Islamic blue dome of *another*, culturally *alien* sheltering sky—this one ornamented with arabesques as *its* transcendental signifieds—within which its protagonists are captured and transformed, as it were, into figures of myth and legend adorning its interior surface.

So, the Orientalist attitudes of projected cultural inferiority onto the East which Port exhibits at the beginning of the narrative of *The Sheltering Sky* dissolve as the narrative proceeds. Indeed, it is precisely the sign regime of Orientalism itself which is being *undone* and *dismantled* by Bowles in his first novel. With the end of the metaphysical age—which I have demarcated in *Art After Metaphysics* as taking place around the time of World War II[95]—the transcendental signifieds of the grand metanarratives which supported, anchored and made that age possible—from Plato to Husserl— are in full, and complete, disintegration. Bowles in 1949 was already anticipating the coming of Derridean deconstruction, for in Derrida's 1966 essay "Structure, Sign and Play in the Discourse of the Human Sciences," he announced that precisely *those* signifieds at the center of Western Being were gone, and therefore that the semiotic *play* of signification—which is potentially infinite, since it is no longer controlled by signifieds—could now be allowed to take their place.[96] Any signifier, in other words, can now point to *any* other signified. *The Sheltering Sky* is already prefiguring Derrida's conclusions.

For without those transcendental siginifeds at the center of Western Being, the protagonists of *The Sheltering Sky* are immunologically *unprotected* and therefore absolutely *anything* can happen to them. Port is physically destroyed like Osiris or Tammuz, while Kit's mind is shattered by an ordeal that is too difficult for her to assimilate within the framework of her own culture, where room for bridal abduction simply does not exist as a behavioral pattern.

Thus, Bowles is not only forecasting the coming of the decolonialization process—which he explores more fully in his third novel *The Spider's House*—but he is also, perhaps, forecasting the humiliation of the West at the hands of the East at some unspecified time in the future (9/11 is still, perhaps, too early), when a "Post-American society" (Fareed Zakaria's term) will rise up and dismantle the West, just as the barbarian hordes of the fifth century took down the Western Roman Empire.

Bowles's novel is essential reading for understanding the beginnings of postwar contemporary literature, for he is already well aware of the coming of the kinds of nihilism—the "absolute darkness" beyond the blue dome of the sky—which will soon be creating the semiotic vacancies that will make morally questionable behavior patterns possible. Indeed, the protagonist of his second novel, Dyar, in *Let it Come Down*, is already a specimen from this post-metaphysical age in which moral signifieds no longer exist to guide and civilize human actions. Dyar is a bank teller from New York City who decides to move to Tangier, and in the process is gradually corrupted: he becomes a thief, rapes a woman and then murders his Arab friend by driving a nail through his ear with a hammer at the novel's conclusion.

Thus, with the "sheltering sky" gone, the hammer of fate now comes down upon anyone unfortunate enough to stray into the path of its descending arc.

(2015)

Heidegger vs. Coca-Cola

The American Mythos

The American mythos: a hypersphere composed of flat, two-dimensional icons that have replaced the transcendental signifieds of the metaphysical age with floating signifiers unanchored and untethered to any kind of semiotic machines. These signifiers only refer to each other in an endless, vast swarm of logos, advertisements and icons that proliferate with viral rapidity and lack any originating *archai*. This hypersphere is composed exclusively of clones and mass-produced objects which self-replicate without telos and without morphological development. That is to say, they are never evolving *into* something, but always only *are* like the vast self-luminous billboards of the city in *Blade Runner*.

As a signifier, nothing metonymizes the rise and spread of this particular American mythos across the planet as does Coca-Cola, the first truly global soft drink. It is a signifier that emerges at the birth of the post-Civil War age of American inauthenticity, Walter Benjamin's mass-produced object which leeches the aura from an original, except that with

Coke, there *is* no original to leech the aura from, a point which Andy Warhol, with his famous Coke bottle paintings will later come to celebrate. The invention of Coke, furthermore, is already a harbinger of the value conflicts of the coming mass wars of the twentieth century, as is foreshadowed in this comment quoted by Heidegger from a letter written by Rilke in 1925:

"To our grandparents, a "house," a "well," a familiar steeple, even their own clothes, their cloak *still* meant something infinitely more, were infinitely more intimate—almost everything a vessel in which they found something human already there, and added to its human store. Now there are intruding, from America, empty indifferent things, sham things, *dummies of life*...A house, as the Americans understand it, an American apple or a winestock from over there, have *nothing* in common with the house, the fruit, the grape into which the hope and thoughtfulness of our forefathers had entered..."[97]

And so the genealogy of Coca-Cola, the first truly mass-produced product—after the printed book, that is—will give us some sense of how the "unworlding" process works, for the planet is currently enclosed on the inside of an empty phase space of deworlded and floating signifiers that are crashing and colliding into one another in the absence of the more ancient transcendental signifieds—i.e. gods, Crucifixion, Apocalypse—which, once upon a time, anchored it to the Infinite and Eternal. The world is a floating world now, adrift with escaped signifiers that refer to other escaped signifiers, but nothing beyond them. Indeed, Heidegger's "Nothing" that he opposed to "Being"[98] hangs over it all like the empty vacuum that used to be imagined to exist beyond the Ptolemaic cosmology of spheres within spheres, the vacuum that lay beyond even the Empyrean.

On the Genealogy of Coca-Cola

To proceed, then, by rewinding: Coke was invented in 1886 by a pharmacist named Dr. John Stith Pemberton as a non-alcoholic beverage that could be sold during the Prohibition movement that had just begun in Atlanta, Georgia, where Pemberton lived (Atlanta, in fact, was the first city to go dry under Prohibition).[99] Pemberton had earlier marketed a drink called "French Wine Coca" which, in addition to its alcoholic content contained a significant amount of cocaine: 0.12 grains cocaine per fluid ounce.[100] With Prohibition in effect, Pemberton dropped the wine, retained the caffeine and added two new ingredients: kola nuts and damiana. Kola nuts, in particular, were then the rage—imported from Ghana—since they contained more caffeine than either tea or coffee.[101]

Pemberton, it should be noted, was a pharmacist and a chemist who was addicted to morphine, and his son was alcoholic, so he may have had a personal interest in using the product as a cure for his own addiction.[102]

When Prohibition put a dent in the sales of his French Wine Coca, he began experimenting with adding various essential oils, primarily distillations of fruit flavors. But these were all too bitter and so he had to add sugar in order to mask the bitterness. Since the result was still too sugary, he added citric acid to counteract the sweetness. But once he had perfected his formula, his business partner Frank Robinson came up with the euphonious name of "Coca-Cola" since such names were in vogue at the time, i.e. Botanic Blood Balm, Copeland's Cholera Cure, etc. etc.[103] Robinson also perfected the product's name as written in Spencerian script, which appeared for the first time in an ad in June of 1887.

Some unknown individual was served the first Coke at a soda fountain in May of 1886 (for five cents) in Jacob's Pharmacy in Atlanta.[104] In its earliest incarnation, Coke was sold in bottles as a syrup that had to be mixed with water. The label read: "Take a tablespoonful in wine glass of water for the relief of headache and nervous afflictions, neuralgia, hysteria, melancholia, etc. A brain tonic and nerve stimulant."[105] Soon after, a druggist began mixing the syrup with carbonated water as a soda fountain drink, and this became the preferred form of taking it.[106]

The first advertisement for Coke appeared in the May 29, 1886 issue of the *Atlanta Journal*, which read: "Coca-Cola, Delicious! Refreshing! Exhilarating! Invigorating! The new and popular soda fountain drink containing the properties of the wonderful Coca plant and the famous Cola nut." Early ads in general proclaimed it as a cure all, insisting that it "Cures Headaches" or "Relieves Mental and Physical Exhaustion."[107]

The drink thus emerged out of a *medical environment* with associations of sickliness and nervous anxiety. Indeed, it was marketed in such contexts up until about 1910, whereupon the imagery of the ads shifted from an aura of the sickly to being associated with strong, vital robust people who are happy and well-adjusted. Thus, from 1886 to 1910, Coke was promoted in an environment that was associated with the nervous, the debilitated, the moody, those who were slightly out of social adjustment which the ads implied could be fixed with the proper dosage of Coca Cola, the same way anti-depressants such as Xoloft and Paxil are marketed today. One ad, for instance, shows a student sitting alone in his armchair with a glass of Coke in one hand while studying. The tagline for the ad reads: "Rx: For Students and all Brain Workers Take one glass Coca-Cola at eight to keep the brain clear and mind active until eleven."[108] Here, the context is unambiguously pharmaceutical.

When Coke was first introduced, it was part of a centralized urban agglomeration that was shifting after the Civil War from an agrarian world of farmers to a settled world of cities connected by complex railroad networks. Railroads, as McLuhan pointed out, tend to have a centralizing effect upon cities, for many of the first department stores were actually transformed train depots. The popularity of the soda fountain, where Coke was first sold, was linked with this horse and buggy carriage world of cities dominated by the railroad.

With the advent of the automobile, however, things changed because cars have an inherently *de*-centralizing effect upon cities (again according to McLuhan), and along with the automobile came a shift *away* from soda fountains toward the bottling of Coke (first bottled in 1894) for a newly nomadic society. The drink's portability was linked with the rise of this society powered by internal combustion engines. Thus, the delocalization of Coke from the soda fountain via the automobile was part of the way in which it spread throughout the world to become the first planetary product.[109]

Coke, then, is the South's victory over the North. It is the response of the South to the disease of general nervous anxiety inflicted onto the human being by the processes of Industrialization, the same processes for which the North fought and won. Thus, the effects upon the nervous system of the highly routinized and mechanized industrial society were already in evidence 21 years after the Civil War. Coke is the Southern response to the machine and to the mechanization of human life generally: a little pep, a little kick-start to the nervous system to get it going again with a tiny dose of cocaine, caffeine and sugar. Hence, note the formula: drugs, stimulants and energetic substances to counteract the debilitating effects of the machine, substances prescribed to adjust the individual to fit more perfectly between the gears of the wheels that are in process of grinding him to pieces. Coke is the Southern oil with which to lubricate the human resources for the Northern megamachines. It is therefore a product inherently designed to promote anonymity, since it specializes in "backgrounding" the potentially—and, in this new machinic world, anarchically—foregrounded individual with all his nervous tics and idiosyncrasies.

Thus, by 1895, Coke was sold in every state and territory of the United States. By 1897, it was sold in Canada, Hawaii and Mexico. By 1900, it had reached London, and by 1912, it was the single best advertised product in the U.S. Coke was the world's first global mass-produced icon, and it soon became *the* icon to be identified with membership in a new kind of society, one that had not been seen on the earth before: a "worldless" society that was on the rise, made possible by capitalism as the ultimate fulfillment of Heidegger's "unworlding" of the West by science, for a "worldless" society is one which is denuded of the local and the authentic, a world full of "non-places" in which every city looks like every other one, and where a world of shopping malls, freeways, fast food restaurants and chain stores dominates over all. Coke was the annunciation, the descending Gabriel, as it were, that announced to the planet the coming victory of the satellization of the earth by technology in which we are now living.

Heidegger and the Unworlding Process

For Heidegger, the West has undergone what he calls the process of "unworlding," especially since the time of Descartes. The primary culprit of this unworlding process is Western science, for science, according to Heidegger, devivifies the world and dehistoricizes the "I," transforming it into a merely theoretical "I," like Husserl's Transcendental Ego or Descartes' *res cogitans*.[110]

Descartes was the first to put the world inside of a grid, so that the trajectory of each object could be mapped and charted in accordance with the x and y axes of analytical geometry. The entire world of nature in this view becomes *res extensa*, the world of things extended in space, while the individual human self is *res cogitans*, basically a self-sufficient thinking entity that is set over and against this exterior world. The world is thus unworlded, or as Heidegger puts it, deprived of its worldhood,[111] because it is quantified, mapped and measured on a grid. It is full of self-sufficient substances with attributes, each object being capable of precise naming and its whereabouts notated on a grid. Even the human being, in this Cartesian transformation, is but a machine with a soul driving it.

In the earlier Medieval understanding of "world," on the other hand, Being was identified with a single entity: God. The ultimate ground of truth, which was based on a correspondence theory, was the agreement between what was held in the mind and the object it contemplated (*adaequatio intellectus ad rem*). But the ultimate guarantor of the truth of anything whatsoever was the notion that the mind of God was the transcendent grounding for all things true: something was true because it was *in* the mind of God, the originating source of all Being. As Heidegger puts it: "In

113

relation to God everything is true insofar as each *res* is only a *veritas* insofar as its being-true is grounded on the fact that it is itself related to the *intellectus divines*."[112]

Thus, the entire world is in some way a function of the mind of God, that being who is thought to be the ultimate source and guarantor of all Being. This is another way of saying that up until about the fifteenth century, men did not hold that their ideas originated in their own minds, but that their thoughts were divine inspirations that originated in the minds of deities. Descartes discovers, however, that his thoughts are indubitably his own and originate within himself, with the sole exception of the idea of God, the perfect being, from whom such an idea has been planted in his brain. By the time of Descartes, God is being pushed out of the picture and relegated to guaranteeing only the verity of a single notion, that namely of the creator himself.

Technology, for Heidegger, poses a threat even to Being itself, for now, for the first time, we live in an age in which Being is no longer identified with a single entity, as it has been since Plato's elevation of Being with the Good as *the* transcendental Form. Being, nowadays, is rather that particular set of hidden cultural assumptions which make anything in the world intelligible as such; indeed, which make a world what it is: *a* world. It is the job of poets and artists, according to Heidegger, to make these hidden assumptions of Being visible for us. Science on the other hand covers them up with its own particular understanding of Being as Enframing (*Gestell*) in which the world is simply the sum total of resources on hand which can be extracted from the earth and stored up to be ready for future use as needed.[113] This particular understanding of Being has covered up all other understandings of Being, and so the role of the artist in such an age is particularly important for rendering obsolete and archaic modes of being (or what Jean Gebser would call structures of consciousness) visible as still extant and accessible.

But now the problem with technology, for Heidegger, is that it levels the world off into a worldless world in which all things, including people, are reified and turned into objects. Nothing is any different from anything else, for all exists as a potential resource to be stored and used. Human beings, in this conception, dissolve into an anonymous mass, *das Man*, as Heidegger terms it, in which no one is essentially distinguishable from anyone else. People become mere things, no different from any other thing, indeed no different even from machines[114] (which we have seen was already the case for Descartes). They thus become "inauthentic," for they are traitors to their own essential nature as Daseins, the mode of being proper to the human being.

In *Being and Time*, Heidegger distinguishes between three different modes of being which are useful to keep in mind here:

Vorhandenheit—(present at hand)[115] this is the mode of being in which objects are thought of as self-sufficient entities existing independently from everything else. This is the ontology of the world since Plato and Aristotle, in which "world" is the sum total of substances with attributes and subjects against objects.

Zuhandenheit—(ready to hand)[116] this is the mode of being proper to tools and machines. Objects are not just theoretical entities here; they are *used* for something. A hammer, for instance, is not just some perceptual object with certain qualities, as it might have been for Husserl, but a tool specifically used for hammering things. And not only that, but it exists in a web of referentiality with other objects. Every object *refers* to something else. When an object breaks, however, it becomes conspicuous *as an object*, for its use value thus comes into question. It stands out from the background of referentiality within which it was embedded and is now in the mode of *Vorhandenheit.*

Dasein—[117]This is the mode of being proper to human beings, and it simply means "being there," although with certain very specific connotations. For a human being to be "there" means that the person is always already engaged in a particular task in a particular world. We are not just subjects existing like some Kantian transcendental ego separate from the world, but we are already involved *in* the world and already with a particular *understanding* of our world, naïve though this may be. So, "world" for Heidegger does not mean subjects vs. objects, but rather self *plus* world, or self plus *a* particular world. This is the way of being proper to human beings, not plants, trees, hammers or anything else.

So the problem with technology for Heidegger is that it collapses these distinctions and renders the differences between Dasein and things null and void. People, in the scientific vision of the world, *are* things, a mere anonymous mass of corpuscle-humans all blended together and drifting with Brownian motion in a void. This is, however, a betrayal of the essence of humanity that envisions "inauthentic" people who have failed to distinguish themselves as individuals. Everyone does what "one" does in such a view. Everyone thinks what "one" thinks. Everyone drinks what "one" drinks (especially if that product is Coca-Cola).

What Coke, then, *Does*

A turn of the century ad for Coca-Cola shows two couples seated in an early style of automobile each receiving a glass of Coke from a waiter who has come out to serve them from a nearby restaurant designed with a Southern style of architecture.[118] (Gyvel Young-Witzel remarks that this was how the drive-in restaurant was born).[119] Whereas, by contrast with the earlier advertising of Coke that catered to the sickly and the nervous, the present ad implies that it is only successful people (the kind who own expensive toys like pre-Ford era automobiles) who drink Coca-Cola and that maybe if *you* drink it too, some of their success will rub off on you.

Note the shift: the climate of the advertising has actually changed the ontological status of the individual from *fixing* him because his nervous exhaustion caused him to stand out from the overall background of industrialized machinery—the early Coca-Cola neurasthenic was in *Vorhandenheit* mode, like Heidegger's broken hammer—to helping him to *blend* into the overall background and to become a part of the industrial machinery as a smooth-running cog (thus putting him into a *Zuhandenheit* mode, where he no longer stands out but meshes with all the other machines). This, however, is precisely Heidegger's point: the mode of *das Man*, of the They, which he speaks of in *Being and Time* as the mass crowd, treats people as "inauthentic," as mere objects, and they therefore become scarcely distinguishable from tools and machines. The product helps to erase and eliminate the properly "authentic" mode of being human that is achieved through a confrontation with death, with one's finitude, and that causes one to "stand out" from the *Gerede* or mere "chatter" of the They.

117

Coke, from a Heideggerian standpoint, is *not* the Real Thing, for it is a signifier of the world of what Rilke called "dummy objects" that destroy authentic Things by flattening them out into mere objects. Society is taken up into a mass hypersphere in which beings have been abandoned by Being, and themselves have been transformed into mere objects, "shapes without form / shades without color," to put it in the words of T.S. Eliot.

Thus, with a Coke in your hand you become just like everyone else who has a Coke in their hand, a mere entity, consumer X, with no distinguishing properties whatsoever. The world advertised by Coke invites the consumer to participate in the time of the World's Darkening, in which real, authentic Things—works of art, old bridges, hand-made jugs—disappear into the gloomy recesses of concealment, to be replaced by flashy icons which emerge from concealment as luminous, glowing signifiers, only to reveal that they are actually bits of the Nothing which function like pieces on a vast and empty gameboard. Play the game and move the pieces around.

But meaning?

Have a Coke and a Smile.

(2010)

Ted Kaczynski's Technological

Gnosticism:

A Consideration of the Unabomber's

Attack on Industrial Society

Prologue

Whereas Heidegger's attack on the floating signifiers of the Nothing which the consumer society represents was aimed at the Imaginary dream world of capitalism excavated by Walter Benjamin in his massive *Arcades Project* from the point of view of the Symbolic—Lacan's plane, that is, of linguistic signifiers—the Unabomber's literal assault upon the very same world of meaningless objects abandoned by Being took place on the plane of the Real. Ted Kaczynski hurled bombs at Rilke's "dummy objects" precisely by attempting to delete their makers—which in the following essay I term the Socratic Man (borrowing, of course, from Nietzsche)—i.e. the various scientists, engineers and big businessmen who ran and constructed the entire *Vorhandenheit* phase space currently engulfing and "deworlding" the planet that Heidegger was the first to warn us all about.

Thus, the ancient mythological signifieds that we began with—gods, myths and Ideas of the Kantian Reason like the soul, freedom and immortality—have slowly, over the millennia, disintegrated and been replaced by mere billboards, Coca-Cola ads and commercials, all of which adds up to Derrida's world of sliding signifiers which creates the very Liquid Modernity in which nothing *sticks* to anything of Transcendent significance. Hence, we began with the Imaginary and now we end up in the desert of the Real.

But first, a review of Kaczynski's deeds will be in order.

The Bombings

From May, 1978 to April, 1995, Theodore J. Kaczynski—a.k.a. the Unabomber—sent out a total of sixteen bombs to various individuals who were all affiliated in one way or another with science. The bombs killed three people and injured twenty-three others, although some of them were defused and did not explode.

The first bomb, however, was not sent through the mail, but delivered by Kaczynski himself to the University of Illinois Chicago Circle Campus on May 25, 1978. He dropped the package between two parked cars in the lot near the Science and Technology buildings, hoping that a student would pick it up and take it to the post office or else hand deliver it to its addressed target, one E. J. Smith, a professor of rocket science at Rensselaer Polytechnic Institute in Troy, New York. The package was found by Mary Gutierrez who tried to fit it into the mail box but couldn't, so she sent it back to the return address, which was listed as Professor Buckley Crisp, Jr., a professor of computer science at Northwestern

University's Technological Institute. When he received the package, however, Crisp thought it looked suspicious, so he contacted campus security, who sent Terry Marker to inspect it. When Marker opened the package, it exploded, nearly blowing off his right hand. He then contacted the ATF, who filed a report, destroyed the evidence and proceeded to forget about it.[120]

But another bomb showed up at Northwestern University a year later: this one was found by a graduate student named John Harris in the student meeting room at the university's Technological Institute. Harris had noticed a Phillies Cigar box on a table and picked it up, whereupon it exploded, causing him some minor injuries. In his private journal, Kaczynski commented: "I had hoped that the victim would be blinded or have his hands blown off or be otherwise maimed...At least I put him in the hospital, which is better than nothing. But not enough to satisfy me. Well, live and learn. No more match-head bombs. I wish I knew how to get hold of some dynamite."[121]

Kaczynski's third bombing attempt was more ambitious, for on November 15, 1979 he managed to detonate a small bomb onboard American Airlines Flight 444 from Chicago O'Hare International Airport to Washington National. The pilots heard a dull thump and the cabin began filling with smoke, forcing them to land at Dulles International. No one was injured.

This third attempt brought Kaczynski to the attention of the FBI, which began an official investigation with no leads and no clues as to the identity of the bomber. On June 10, 1980, United Airlines president Percy Wood received a package that had been sent from Chicago containing a copy of a book, Sloan Wilson's novel *Ice Brothers*. But behind the title page, the book had been hollowed out to contain a bomb, and when Wood opened the book, it exploded on him, inflicting minor injuries.[122]

At this point, the FBI gave the mysterious serial bomber a name, based on his attempts to send bombs to universities and airlines: the Unabomber, as he would be known to the public from henceforth.

Over the following years, six more bombs were sent to various professors of science and computer engineering, but there were no fatalities until December 11, 1985 when, in Sacramento, California, Kaczynski placed a bomb designed to look like a piece of scrap lumber in the back lot behind a computer repair shop. When the shop's owner, Hugh Scutton, went to pick up the lumber, it exploded, blowing off his hand and rupturing his heart, killing him.

There was an almost identical bombing on February 20, 1987 when another computer store owner, this time in Salt Lake City, picked up a piece of scrap lumber that exploded on him, mangling his left arm, although in this case, he wasn't killed.

Six years then elapsed with no bombing attempts, while Kaczynski, working in his shack in the Montana woods, tried to perfect his bombs and make them more powerful. The results of these experiments were then unleashed on a geneticist, a Dr. Charles Epstein, who lived in the community of Tiburon, California. On June 22, 1993, Dr. Epstein picked up a small package in his house one morning, opened it, and the resulting explosion knocked him backward. He survived the blast, however.

But it wasn't until December 10, 1994, that Kaczynski's second fatality took place, when an executive named Thomas Mosser, who worked for a public relations firm called Burson-Marsteller was killed when he opened a package in the kitchen of his own house. In a letter to the *New York Times* which Kaczynski wrote under the alias of "FC," (an abbreviation for "Freedom Club") in which he pretended that he was a member of an anarchist group, he wrote: "Burston-Marsteller is about the biggest organization in the public relations field. This means that its business is the development of techniques for manipulating people's attitudes. It was for this more than for its actions in specific cases that we sent the bomb to an executive of this company..."[123]

Kaczynski's third and final fatality, as well as his last bomb, came when, on April 24, 1995, he mailed a package to the president of the California Forestry Association in Sacramento, one Gilbert Murray, who opened the package, which exploded on him with such force that the blast literally ripped Murray to pieces.

It was at this point that Kaczynski mailed proposals to three different publications: *Penthouse* magazine, *The New York Times* and *The Washington Post*, in which he offered to stop sending bombs if one of the publications would publish his 30,000 word manifesto entitled "Industrial Society and its Future." The *Post* took him up on the offer, after conferring with the FBI, which advised them that it might help catch Kaczynski by bringing someone forward who was familiar with the writing.

And indeed, when Ted's brother David read the manifesto, he recognized his brother's writing and reluctantly turned him over to the FBI, which arrested him on April 3, 1996.

In exchange for the government's agreement not to seek the death penalty, Kaczynski plead guilty to thirteen federal bombing offenses, and acknowledged responsibility for all sixteen bombings from 1978 to 1995. He is currently serving a life sentence with no possibility of parole.

The Man of Science

The first thing that strikes us about these bombings is their seriality and repetition. They are a *series* of identical-but-different situations—like Andy Warhol's soupcans—in which an effort is made to bomb the Man of Science. It was not sixteen different individuals that Kaczynski was trying to destroy, but rather the *one* Being which these sixteen individuals incarnated: the Platonic archetype of the Scientific Man. Kaczynski, then, was actually trying to destroy a Platonic Form, and the only way to do this is to replicate a *series* of attacks. To counter the One, one must resort to the principle of the Many, for it is precisely through the Many that the One makes itself manifest.

Industrial Society survives—indeed, *flourishes*—based upon the principle of serial repetition through mass production. It is precisely the mass production of basic, undying consumer signifiers which enables it to gain power over the physical world by the sheer force of its swarms of products. Andy Warhol made this clear in his soupcan paintings, which reveal the presence of the Form behind the individual Campbell's soupcans simply by analyzing their principle of repetition. He did the same thing with Coke bottles, Brillo boxes, etc., which unveil for us the basic consumer signifiers: *the* Can of Campbell's Soup, of which all existing cans are merely imperfect copies; *the* bottle of Coke; *the* Brillo Box; and so forth. Master copies made manifest through their repetition.

But now it is precisely by his participation in these chains of seriality that *the* Consumer is created. The Platonic Forms of the consumer society create the ideal Consumer simply by the fact of his participation in the sacrament of buying,

124

consuming, and then *re*-buying and consuming the *same* products *ad inifintum*. In the process, the Consumer himself is cloned and replicated. Indeed, now he is everywhere, ubiquitous, omnipresent throughout all time and space. Industrial Society replicates consumers. We are all consumers who have been cloned and replicated, whether knowingly or not, by the mere fact of our obsessive, repetitive consumption of the same products over time and through space.

But now if it were possible to destroy the Platonic Forms of consumer society (their ersatz signifieds, as it were), then it follows that the individual copies, mass reproduced, would cease to appear. And if the endless seriality and repetition of its products was halted, then the Consumer would cease to exist, for there would be no mass produced products for him to participate in through their consumption. We would all then be forced to become *singularities*, capable of regarding ourselves as clones no longer, but forced to become true individuals ("authentic" in Heidegger's sense). We would have to live our own lives, create our own products, rough-hewn, each one of us in the process becoming an imperfect individuality.

It is precisely the Man of Science, however, who has power over all this magic of production. It is the Man of Science—Nietzsche's Socratic Man, in fact[124]—the man of reasonableness, logic and rationality who, due to his command over the Platonic Secrets—the universal laws and their mathematic formulae—has control over the principles underlying the phenomenal world. His mastery of those Platonic archetypes enables Industrial Society to come into being, to function at all, for the Man of Science is the priest of the machine whose knowledge of the machines makes it all work. Indeed, without his knowledge, there would *be* no machines to mass produce the Consumer Forms. Behind the existence of each and every one of these machines, there lies at its ultimate root just such a Man of Science: behind the automobile engine, for example, there is always a Gottlieb Daimler, a Jean Joseph Lenoir, a Sadi Carnot; men of science, that is, who had mastery over the equations and secrets which they made possible, the secrets for unlocking the existence of the machines and eventually, of their principles of seriality and repetition.

It follows, then, that if you can destroy the archetype of the Man of Science, then Industrial Society would collapse, taking all of its mass production and its endless repetition of clones along with it. The society would disappear, and so too would the Consumer as a type. We would all be forced to become singularities, each one of us an unprecedented human event, forced to create our own microcosms.

Just like Ted Kaczynski, who withdrew from Industrial Society, refused to participate in its principle of seriality and repetition, and decided to rely upon himself to produce his own food, his own house, his own life. A complete singularity unto himself; a *swerving* like Lucretius's *clinamen*, in which the atoms suddenly, unpredictably, swerve from their predetermined course to go their own way through the cosmos.

Hence, the media's caricature of Kaczynski as the bizarre hermit and reclusive loner who, because he did not fit into the mass production of human forms *inside* Industrial Society, seems so strange that he must be mentally ill. After all, only a madman would criticize Industrial Society and choose to become a human singularity.

But then in the microcosmology which Kaczynski created, it is precisely the matter of interiors vs. exteriors that counts. *Inside* Industrial Society, one is a slave; *outside* it, the possibility of Freedom exists as the fruit of the Tree of

Knowledge—hence, his obsession with wood—for those who wish to reach for it.

Technological Gnosticism

In order to understand Kaczynski's principle of interiors vs. exteriors (in which freedom for the individual only exists *outside* of cosmic containers) it is necessary to glance for a moment at his manifesto, in which he explains his motivations for becoming a terrorist.

Kaczynski states that the human individual, in order to attain fulfillment, must normally go through what he calls "the power process," in which he initiates and sets his own goals, expends a significant amount of effort toward the achievement of those goals, and is actually able to accomplish at least some of them.[125] A significant degree of autonomy, then, is necessary for the completion of this task. But he points out that industrial society actually inhibits and interferes with this process because it places the modern human being inside a mesh of impersonal bureaucratic forces which tyrannize over him with demands, regulations and constant stresses. Decisions are made by politicians, bureaucrats and technicians over which the individual has no influence and no say, and these decisions decide a great deal of his fate and destiny, which is thus largely robbed from him. The modern individual *loses* his freedom to control his own circumstances because he is constantly harried by these impersonal technocratic forces upon which he becomes dependent for much of his safety and security. Thus, he has no control over huge portions of his life—such as the guarantee of his own safety, for which he must rely on public officials and government representatives to provide for him (for instance, by ensuring safety regulations at nuclear power plants or making sure

127

that no toxins get into the food or water supplies) and as a consequence, he loses the ability to go through the power process on his own.[126] He is always accountable to *someone else* for his actions—his employer, the government, etc.—and this leads to frustration, anxiety and a sense of unfulfillment. He turns, therefore, to surrogate activities, such as the taking up of a hobby, or a sport like golf or bodybuilding, which are inessential to the needs of his existence.[127]

Technology, furthermore, is constantly forced upon him whether he likes it or not. New gadgets are often introduced at first as conferring new freedoms—such as the automobile, which apparently gave an advantage over the pedestrian—but which soon become mandatory and progressively narrow, and limit, his options (as when the city has to be redesigned to accommodate the automobile, and soon, everyone must have one to survive).[128] Technology imposes its functions upon the hapless individual, who is gradually hemmed in by its demands and soon becomes its prisoner, robbed of his freedoms. The more technologized a society becomes, Kaczynski insists, the fewer freedoms there are. Constitutionally guaranteed freedom is only nominal; in reality, it is the economic and technological structures in a society, not its government, which determine how much freedom the individual has in that society.

Thus, in the cosmology which Kaczynski designs in his manifesto, the modern individual living *inside* industrial society is actually its prisoner. Freedom is an illusion, for technological determinism binds and captures him on all fronts. It is only *outside* industrial society, in the state of what Kaczynski calls "wild nature" that the individual becomes truly free to shape his own life.[129] The individual *inside* industrial society, on the other hand, is fallen and in need of redemption. The only way to rescue him is to destroy and dismantle industrial society, which has long since passed the possibility of reforming. It must be blown apart, and can in no way be saved.

This cosmology of diminished freedom for the individual trapped *inside* a cosmic container, and who can only attain any real kind of freedom on the *outside* of it, bears certain structural similarities to the cosmology of Gnosticism. In the cosmos as it was envisioned by the Gnostics of the first two or three centuries AD, the human individual was also trapped inside a machine, namely the cosmos itself, which had been constructed by malevolent beings known as Archons. Each of these archons was assigned to one of the cosmic spheres containing the seven heavenly bodies which whirled around the earth, a small flat disc which they had created as a prison for human beings. The highest of these archons was a being named Yaltabaoth (the Hebrew Yahweh) whose sphere was that of Saturn, the outermost of the cosmic spheres, and the demiurge who had brought it all into being under the mistaken impression that he was the creator of the cosmos.[130]

The human soul's fate was controlled by something called *Heimarmene*, the Gnostic word for Fate, which was exerted astrologically by the planets and their archons, who had helped to construct the physical world and to imprint the human soul with the archetypal qualities associated with each of the planets, such as Fear, Envy, Jealousy, Wrath, etc. Thus, the archons were the enemies of the soul, whose only escape lay in the possibility of attaining gnosis, or initiation into the cosmic secret that one's true destiny was to attain the realm of Light that lay above and beyond the cosmic spheres, a realm known as the Pleroma, where dwelt the ultimate beings of Light, Sophia and the Aeons, the *true* creators of the cosmos. Gnosis lay in the realization that the human soul was actually a spark of light fallen from this realm and trapped inside a mortal human body subject to astrological determinism. Attainment of true freedom lay in escaping the Gnostic cosmos by ascending through the spheres, battling past the Archons (who were in possession of the archetypal Forms—or Transcendental Signifieds, as Derrida would call them—by way of which the physical world was constructed) and becoming reunited with the Pleroma.

Thus, in the Gnostic cosmos, too, freedom was a matter of escaping from a cosmic container, in this case, the cosmos itself. Once outside the realm of the spheres, the soul's freedom could be attained in the Pleroma, a world that lay *outside* the cosmic machine.

In Kaczynski's cosmos, the astrological determinism of the Gnostics finds its analogue in the technological determinism of Industrial Society. Freedom, likewise, can only be truly attained *outside* this cosmic vessel, not in the Pleroma, but in the state of "wild nature." Kaczynski's war against the scientists is directly analogous to the soul's war against the archons, for the archons, like the scientists, are in possession of the basic archetypal structures that have enabled them to create their respective societies as machines for trapping, and storing, human souls.

Thus, if you can destroy the Man of Science, then the cosmic machine trapping and encasing human souls will collapse in on itself, releasing its horde of caged human beings.

In both systems, then, freedom is lost on the *inside* of their cosmic containers, and regained only in the cosmic wildernesses *outside* them.

Two Kinds of Strategy for Redemption

The hidden Gnostic structures in Kaczynski's narrative actually reveal more about the structures of technological society than they do about the structure of Kaczynski's mind. They show us that modern man is, indeed, fallen—or "thrown" as Heidegger would put it[131]—inside a technological apparatus that has closed up around him and from which he is in need of redemption, but doesn't know it. There are, however, a number of different strategies available for this Fallen Man to avail himself of in order to escape from the Belly of the Beast that has swallowed him up, and Kaczynski's particularly violent approach is only one of them.

Marshall McLuhan, for instance, offered a distinctly different type of strategy with his idea of "escape through understanding." In this case, the individual doesn't rely on a hero to blow a hole into the side of the Beast *for* him, which Kaczynski's approach implies, but rather gives him the tools to save himself. One escapes the clutches of technological determinism on a *psychological* rather than a crudely *physical* level by studying the technological apparatus, and learning to understand its mechanisms of manipulation and control. In thus coming to understand the machine, one is able to escape from the possibility of being manipulated by it.[132] Theodor Adorno, with his study of the Culture Industry in *The Dialectic of Enlightenment*, offers a similar kind of approach.[133]

Kaczynski's analysis of the manipulative nature of technological society is, I think, accurate. The problem with it, though, is that his technological soteriology was so crudely literal. The Gnostics, too, escaped through understanding, for that is what gnosis means, "to know." There is no need to physically blow up industrial society: it will eventually collapse of its own weight, just like the Roman Empire. In the meantime, the individual must achieve gnosis through understanding how and why the civilizational megamachine seeks to control our lives.

Kaczynski's attempt to rescue the fallen human soul through blowing a hole into the side of industrial civilization is simply a rehearsal of the myth of the solar hero who comes to one's rescue *from the outside.* But the approaches of McLuhan, Adorno and Critical Theory are a form of *self-salvation* which can actually be attained by anyone willing to sit down and do the work of reading the texts.

It's too bad that Kaczynski's rage led him to kill people, for his analysis of how Industrial Society manipulates us is interesting to contemplate. Modern man's predicament, I agree, *is* enraging, and needs to be discussed.

But his attack on industrial society is only one more example of the kinds of rage that it is inciting against itself all over the world.

There will be more such attacks, as the decades unfold. Count on it.

(2014)

A Few (More) Words on

Thomas Pynchon's 1963 Novel *V.*

Incipit

Thomas Pynchon's 1963 first novel *V.* is not so much a novel as a series of short novels held together by hinges: the book is composed of 17 chapters (or 16 + an epilogue), seven of which are short novels having to do with the mysterious woman known as "V" while the other chapters function as jointures—like Heidegger's jointures in his *Contributions to Philosophy*[134]—which hinge the other seven together. Thus, the book is meant to be symbolically "unfolded" and opened up in a manner similar to the way in which the wings of a Medieval triptych—also hinged—are opened to reveal a series of panels, each chronicling one or another Biblical iconotype. (Van Eyck's Ghent Altarpiece of about 1430 is a classic example).

The story is composed of two narrative arcs: the main picture panels—as it were—associated with the attempts of one Herbert Stencil to fathom the mystery of the woman named V., while the other is composed of the random and chaotic motions of a group of artists and beatniks who call themselves the Whole Sick Crew. Benny Profane, though he has no talents whatsoever to speak of, is the main character associated with this arc, who bounces from job to job and from lover to lover in an endless sequence of hilarious episodes. At one point, in a mock heroic miniaturization of the dragon-slayer myth, Pynchon has him hired on to hunt alligators in the New York sewer system.

Stencil and Profane, between them, then, rehearse the Western philosophical dialectic of the intelligible vs. the sensible worlds, for Stencil, as his name implies, is always sifting through texts looking for meaning, projecting his various theoretical templates onto world history in order to make sense out of it, while Profane—again as the name implies—couldn't care less about anything, and simply drifts from one aimless adventure to the next, absolutely unaware of the presence of the Higher Mind and all its attempts to translate mere empirical experience into the transcendence of systems of meaning and order. Whereas Stencil yearns for the transcendence of dissolution into the body of the Great Mother, Profane remains a lost and alienated fragment of contemporary consciousness mired in the sense data of the fallen world.

Together, then, they compose the mind and senses of the human physical body in both its animal and suprahuman modalities. If V. as modern incarnation of the Great Mother is the physical body, they are the twin components of the senses and intellect which inhabits it in the form of an animate human soul.

The two narrative arcs of the novel therefore trace out their own letter "V" which only come together when Stencil and Profane join forces near the novel's conclusion in order to travel to the island of Malta, where Stencil thinks he might actually meet the woman named V. in person. Needless to say, this doesn't happen, for at the novel's end Stencil is off to Europe to pursue another clue, while Profane drifts into yet another love entanglement that we know isn't going to get him anywhere, since Pynchon has gone to great pains to detail for the reader how incapable of love Profane really is.

It is a novel, in other words, without an Event, in either the Heideggerian or Badiouan senses of the term. (For Alain Badiou, an event creates a subject through the subject's fidelity to a happening of truth, such as quantum physics or the French Revolution;[135] whereas for the later Heidegger, Being itself is an event in which entities are unconcealed in the Clearing in a new way, by poets or thinkers or artists, which sets up new parameters of intelligibility for the Clearing of the culture as a whole).

The Quest for V.

Herbert Stencil is a sort of scholar who is obsessed with solving the mystery of the identity of a woman whose first initial, V., appears in his father's journals. His father Sidney was a spy for the British government at the turn of the century, a fact which places Herbert in the tradition of the literary sleuth who gathers clues for the reader to assemble into causal sequence in order to solve a crime. V. may, in fact, be Stencil's mother; he doesn't know for sure. But then, he doesn't know *anything* for certain. He is a middle-aged man who spends his time poring through texts and historical documents, such as letters and journals, interviewing people who may or may not have known this woman, seeking to uncover her identity. He never finds out, though, just exactly *who* she is, since every time her name comes up, it has changed: at first, it is Victoria Wren; later it becomes Veronica Manganese, Vera Meroving and, at one point, even Veronica the Rat. He is never even certain of her name: only that it begins with the twenty-second letter of the alphabet.

Each of the seven mini-novels—which are all constructions of Stencil's, based on his research—takes place at a moment of historical crisis. The first one is set in 1898 during the so-called Fashoda crisis, in which the British and the French nearly went to war over their respective colonialist claims in Egypt. V. first appears there in the guise of the young woman named Victoria Wren, the girlfriend of a spy named Goodfellow. She also has an eleven year old sister named Mildred, who has a penchant for collecting rocks, minerals and fossils, a fact not unconnected with V.'s later fate (although we never hear of Mildred again).

The third of the mini-novels—after a short one involving an insane priest who tries to convert rats in the New York sewers into his flock—takes place in Florence in 1899, where V. appears once again as Victoria Wren, only now associated with a plot to steal Botticelli's painting *The Birth of Venus* from the Uffizi gallery. But the plot is entangled with the politics of a Venezuelan uprising, during which Victoria listens to the story of a man named Hugh Godolphin—loosely modeled on H. Rider Haggard's Allan Quatermain—who tells her of his journeys to a mysterious land known as Vheissu (a Pynchon joke on "*Wie heisst du?*" or "What is your name?")[136] that vaguely resembles myths of Shambhala, and of his journey to the South Pole where he encountered, frozen in the ice at the pole, an upside down spider monkey (in place of which Dante, the first to travel through the earth's core, found Satan hanging like a bat upside down). Godolphin insists to his listener that the spider monkey meant Absolutely Nothing and indeed, mocked all attempts at meaning, a sort of cosmic joke at his expense.

136

It thus becomes apparent to the reader very early on that the letter "V" is a sliding signifier in Pynchon's narrative, a signifier which could refer to the various signifieds of Victoria Wren, Vheissu, Venus, Vesuvius or even Venezuela. As Jacques Derrida might point out, the letter V is a signifier whose meaning is uncontrolled by any firm anchorage to a Transcendental Signified, and it has therefore come loose, as it were, from any apparatus of semiotic capture and gone sliding across the pages of Pynchon's book, constantly deferring and differing in its meaning wherever it appears. It has become a mere trace that is left over from the logocentric age in which its meaning would have been fixed and captured in some binary system of metaphysical origin.[137] But Pynchon's V. is an escaped signifier running amok through his narrative.

In the fourth mini-novel, which is set in South Africa in 1922, a story which Stencil recounts to a dentist named Eigenvalue (in the mode of Conrad's Marlow recounting one of his long tales to a pipe-smoking listener as the evening sun melts into the horizon), V. surfaces as one Vera Meroving, a woman with a glass eye that has a tiny clock face painted onto its iris, during a revolt of the Bondel tribesmen against their German oppressors. The episode is somewhat of a replay of an earlier historical episode set in 1904, during which the Germans brutally suppressed a revolt of the Herrero tribesmen in one of their South African colonies, genocidally exterminating most of the tribesmen. Here, the revolt of the Bondel tribesmen fares somewhat better, and the mini-novel's protagonist, Kurt Mondaugen, an electrical engineer who witnesses the revolt, heads for the hills and disappears at the end.

In the fifth mini-novel, this time set during the bombing raids on the island of Malta during World War II, and known as a diary entitled "The Confessions of Fausto Mai-jstral," which Stencil gives (or recounts) to Benny Profane, the woman named V. turns up as an even more mysterious personage known only as the Bad Priest. She drifts around Malta giving anti-Catholic sermons to groups of gathered children, who listen to her with bemusement. During a bombing raid, a building collapses upon her, and the children find her there, pinned beneath the rubble: by this point, she has become a veritable cyborg and they make off with her prosthetic feet, her glass eye, the sapphire sewn into her navel, and a set of false teeth in which each tooth is made out of a different precious metal.

She may, or may not have died in this rubble, but Stencil sets off, toward the novel's conclusion, together with his *schlemihl* companion Benny Profane, to modern day Malta (in 1956, during yet another historical crisis, in this case that of the Suez Crisis) in order to find her. He has managed to convince Profane to steal the set of metallic teeth from the dentist Eigenvalue (who had somehow inherited it), and Stencil intends to give them to her as a present. Of course, when they get to the island, Stencil finds nothing but "traces" left behind by V.'s absence and more clues, which send him off on yet another quest for answers, while Profane entangles himself in another pointless love affair.

There are two other mini-novels concerning V—such as one that takes place in Paris in July of 1913, just before the outbreak of World War I, in which she is known as the "Lady V.," who falls in love with a ballerina—but the key thing about each one is that it is set during a moment of historical crisis. Indeed, V. has a knack for turning up at just those moments in the history of Western civilization in which collective violence is about to break out.

And she turns up, furthermore, in each of these contexts, as they evolve over time, with more and more of her anatomy having fused with what Pynchon in the novel terms the "Inanimate." In 1898, it is only her sister Mildred who is concerned with collecting bits of the Inanimate in the form of fossils and shells; in 1899 V. has an ivory comb in the shape of a line of crucified British soldiers in her hair; and in 1913, she already has the glass eye, as well as a sapphire sewn into her navel; by 1943, she is a cyborg complete with prosthetic appendages, tattoos and various bits of the Inanimate fused with her physical flesh. The mini-novels, in other words, whatever their Truth value—since they come from unreliable sources and narrators—tell the story of V.'s descent into mechanization, a descent that most deliberately parallels the West's descent as a whole into total mechanization and automation throughout the course of the twentieth century. It is, furthermore, not an accident that this increasing technologization of the West occurs in tandem with scenes of historical violence, since Pynchon is implying that the West's mechanization has only contributed to brutalizing its sensibilities.

On the one hand, the letter V may be a floating signifier in the narrative, where it can signify all sorts of things (its meaning, therefore, cannot be precisely pinned down), but on the other hand, the woman V. herself, as an image, actually *is* a Transcendental Signified: namely, the Muse of Western Civilization, who has gone by many names.

And one of those names, of course, is the Virgin.

Virgo / Virgin

So, one of the things that Pynchon is doing in this novel is what I would term a "recoding" of the goddess of Western

Civilization, i.e. the Virgin Mary, into a sort of Muse of the Machine. Henry Adams, in his autobiography (which we know Pynchon read) insisted in the chapter entitled "The Dynamo and the Virgin" that the hall of dynamos that he stood in awe before at the Great Exhibition in Chicago of 1893 was a contemporary equivalent of the same power, force and majesty of the cult of the Virgin that, during the Middle Ages, brought all the great cathedrals into being. The electrical dynamo, in other words, had, for Adams, replaced the Virgin as the primary symbol for the age.[138]

Indeed, we can go even further than Adams and say that the Virgin, in essence, *was* the cathedral, which functioned in those days as a mighty apparatus of semiotic capture: if you cracked open a cathedral, what you found inside were the various components of saints, altars, niches and stained glass windows. If you were to cut open the body of Pynchon's V., on the other hand, you would find diodes, cathode tubes, transistors and various mechano-electric components. The primary apparatus of semiotic capture for each age, then, has shifted from the Virgin to V., a.k.a. the Mechanical Bride, as McLuhan dubbed her.[139] Pynchon has taken the Virgin as the West's most important Transcendetal Signified and re-coded, or reterritorialized her to become the Mistress of the Inanimate as Machine. Today's revelation is not the cathedral, but the Machine as a world unto itself.

Indeed, this recoding or reterritorializing of the goddess has taken place before in the history of the West, several times, in fact. In an earlier incarnation, she was known to the Egyptians as Isis, the mother of the young child Horus, whom she kept on her lap exactly as the Virgin is later depict-ed with the Christ child on her lap. Indeed, the Byzantines, around the year 600 took Isis with the Horus child directly from the sands and broken temples of Egypt (the temple of

Isis at Philae was shut down in 560 AD and reconsecrated to the Virgin) to become one of the main iconotypes of Byzantine art, just as that art itself had been a reterritorialization of the Roman art of painting funerary portraits on Egyptian coffins in places like the Faiyum in the 4th and 5th centuries. The anonymous individuals of those funerary portraits gradually became, as Hans Belting in his book *Likeness and Presence* has described it, the various saints and Biblical figures comprising the matter of Byzantine icon painting.[140]

So, that was the first reterritorialization of the goddess, in which Isis became Mother Mary, the blue of whose robes was associated with the heavenly vault, just as the red in those same robes became the blood of Christ mapped onto the setting sun in that very same heavenly sky.

After the Fourth Crusade of 1204 AD, the West began to import the art of the Byzantine icons in vast profusion. The iconotype of the Virgin with the Christ child on her lap became the main iconotype (or as Derrida would prefer "Transcendental Signified") of that age. The body of the Virgin was inflated to the size of a Gothic cathedral, inside which Christ on the Cross became an embryo. And just as Christ was imagined as being on the *inside* of his Mother's body, so we too, as worshippers, were contained in Her womb.

But the Virgin was recoded once again during the Renaissance of the 15th century when, with the discovery of the laws of perspectival space, the tiny, dollhouse miniature world of the previous art went down the drain and took most of the Medieval iconotypes with it. The Virgin, however—together with God Himself—managed to survive into the new age in which the primary Transcendetal Signified became that of Infinite Space. The Virgin was recoded by Leonardo in his 1504 *Mona Lisa* ("Mona" is a contraction

141

of "Madonna") as the Mistress of Infinite Space, for the key thing about Leonardo's painting isn't so much the woman in the foreground as the backdrop of Infinite Space behind her that nearly swallows her up. Other painters, such as Isenbrandt in his 1510 (or so) *Rest on the Flight Into Egypt* or Gerard David's 1515 version of this same theme, soon follow Leonardo by setting the actual Virgin back into a quaint landscape with distant horizons and vanishing points suggestive of the absolute Infinity of Endless Space, the new Signified of the later metaphysical age.[141]

Thus, Pynchon's recoding of the Virgin in his first novel *V.* as the Mistress now, not of Infinite Space—for that disintegrated with Impressionism—but of the Inanimate, or the Machine, is but one in a series of reterritorializings of this goddess of Western civilization who is still among us, found most conspicuously as McLuhan identified her in our magazine ads as the Mechanical Bride. In the imagery of science fiction films and novels, of course, she has, since Fritz Lang's 1927 film *Metropolis*, turned up everywhere. The Muse has not so much learned to write, as Eric Havelock would have it,[142] but how to inspire men to make machines as little microcosmic wonders upon earth, revelations of her infinite power.

And so, one of the vectors, anyway, of Pynchon's novel is to chronicle this transformation of Western sensibilities from an orientation to the possibilities of Infinite Space to the possibility of Infinite Machines.

The Problem of "Truth"

But, of course, there still remains that problem in Pynchon's narrative with Truth. For all of Stencil's texts and documents which he uses to reconstruct the history of V. are questionable, and seem to contain distortions, exaggerations and rumors. The floating signifier of the V becomes associated in these documents with so many things—places, people, entities—that the reader, after a while, begins to question the very value of what Stencil is up to. Perhaps he is merely paranoid. Perhaps there is no V. except only in the mind of Herbert Stencil. We can never know for sure.

This aspect of Pynchon's narrative is what marks his novel as a thoroughly postmodern one, for the more Stencil examines V. through all his collecting and gathering of documents—like Isis trying to find all the pieces of the scattered body of Osiris—the further she recedes from his grasp, and the more doubts the reader has about his quest. But this perfectly parallels Gadamer's insistence, in his 1960 work of philosophy called *Truth and Method*, that there is no such thing as the text-in-itself—just as, according to Kant, the thing-in-itself is forever out of our reach because all our knowledge is predetermined in advance by the limitations of the mind's faculties—for the text, as an objective understanding of its author's original intentions, cannot ever be fully reconstructed. Historical layers of preconceptions and biases of each age get in the way of reaching any such purely objective understanding, and so all knowledge of the text, for Gadamer, is merely a function of each age's attempt to understand the text anew.[143] There *is* no text-in-itself, and so there *is* no objective Truth.

Gadamer's conclusions are, of course, a direct application of Heidegger's revolutionary theory of truth as *aletheia*, in which truth shifts from a correspondence theory of ideas matching facts, to a matter of degrees of unconcealment of entities in what he calls "the Clearing." There is no such thing as a merely binary understanding of truth for Heidegger, since every entity that unconceals itself for us in this

Clearing—his term for the intellectual space of encounter between entities in a civilization—does so by showing us only partial aspects of itself, while other aspects simultaneously withdraw into concealment. Every question we put to an entity causes certain of its aspects to unconceal themselves to us, but at the same time, other aspects not addressed by those particular questions fall off the radar, where they remain concealed in the dark matter of Being.[144] (Awaiting, perhaps, the day in which the proper questions will be asked of them that will pull them forth into unconcealment).

This is simply the nature of Truth in the postmodern age. It is an exact equivalent, in philosophy, of the attempt to measure particles in quantum theory. Every measurement, in Heisenberg's Uncertainty Principle, actually disturbs the particle in such a way that it is impossible ever to get a fully "objective" reading of both position and speed of the particle at the same time.

And so, Stencil's attempt, likewise, to unconceal the mystery of V. through his various texts and documents causes her to recede and withdraw ever more thoroughly away from his grasp. V. thus becomes a symbol for Truth in the post-metaphysical age of Heidegger and Gadamer. She *is* a Heideggerian entity withdrawing into concealment in the Clearing, precisely in proportion to how many questions Stencil puts to her. The more we ask of her, the less we know.

And this is a phenomenon that recurs throughout all of Pynchon's texts, a phenomenon we might call "Pynchon's Paradox."

Goddess

Finally, from a media studies viewpoint, let us not forget that the title of Pynchon's first novel is not "*V*" but rather

"*V.*" with a period typed after the twenty-second letter of the alphabet. The font and typeface looks exactly like the letter V as typed by a typewriter, a machine that rendered the Gutenbergian printing press portable so that, as McLuhan put it in *Understanding Media*, the typewriter enabled both composition and publication to take place simultaneously during the writer's creative process.[145] Thus, the title refers to the fact that it was the Semitic alphabet that made possible the unfolding of letters into moveable type during the 15th century when the printing press was invented as a means of mechanizing the composition of books.

But the alphabet, as Vilem Flusser pointed out, (or rather alphabetic writing) was part of a gobbling up of the mythic world of images by their organization into commentaries in rows of lines of one-dimensional text by the Greeks and the Hebrews, who invented alphabetic writing as a means of criticizing and analyzing and breaking mythical images apart into pieces[146] (just as V. in Pynchon's narrative has fallen, like Humpty Dumpty, from the wall and shattered into the various pieces which Stencil is attempting to put back together again). The alphabet was a machine for chewing up images—indeed, the interior row of metal keys of a typewriter resembles nothing so much as a mouth full of teeth (witness the giant insect with a typewriter for a mouth in David Cronenberg's *Naked Lunch*)—and gave rise to the texts of the scientific age (along with its correspondence theory of truth as the *adequatio* of ideas with things).

But in the post-Gutenbergian (McLuhan), posthistoric (Flusser) world of today, writing and linearity have been scaled down and peripheralized by the rise of electric media such as the television and the computer. The visual sense which printed writing favors in abstraction from all other senses has been stepped down, while the acoustic and tactile senses have been stepped up. Thus, the acceleration into light speed causes a reversal of letters back into the sculptural, tactile and mythic qualities of the iconic.

Pynchon, in his novel *V.*, transforms the twenty-second letter of the alphabet into an icon, in a way that is perfectly consistent with his age's shift into posthistoric imagistic media. "V" the alphabetic letter has become associated with the ancient mythical signified of the Virgin goddess, and so the letter V can best be visualized as standing in a landscape on a horizon as a gigantic sculpture casting its own shadow on the ground before it (as depicted, in fact, on the novel's original paperback cover put out by Bantam). V., in Pynchon's narrative, that is to say, has taken on the tactile and imagistic qualities of a mythical icon, like a Byzantine Madonna. It is a letter of the alphabet no more.

The letter V is, of course, an archaic Paleolithic inscription for the *mons pubis* above the goddess's vaginal cleft (Pynchon registers this symbolism by organizing the synopsis at the top of each chapter heading in the shape of a pubic triangle). It is one of the oldest written symbols in the world, a hieroglyphic abbreviation for the power of the Great Mother and existed as such long before the Hebrews killed the goddess and turned her symbol into the abstract alphabetic letter called "*vav.*"[147]

Pynchon reclaims from the Hebrews the ancient iconic symbol of the goddess and so reading his novel becomes tantamount to a journey through the world interior of her anatomy, as though she formed the novel's apparatus of semiotic capture, just like one of those cathedrals of the Middle Ages. The chapters and mini-novels thus become the various structures of her internal anatomy.

But now the Great Mother returns at the end of the metaphysical age, having been recoded within the paternal

146

womb that began with Plato and the Greek and Hebrew gods—from whose heads sprang goddesses like Athena, or Eve from Adam's rib—as a paternalized signifier whose anatomy has become encrusted with the Platonic Ideas of gadgets and prostheses. It is not quite the Great Mother anymore, for she has had to suffer the indignity of being reterritorialized by the Platonic Ideas of the paternal womb, and now finds herself as a sort of hybrid or synthesis of maternal and paternal components.

The paternal technologies of Father Science—already fathomed by Mary Shelley in her brilliant novel *Frankenstein* in 1818—have tried to replace her: now we have in vitro fertilization, test tube babies, cloning and GMO foods that have come from the womb of the male mind as technologized attempts to replace the "natural" processes of her great chthonic bounty.[148]

But then, of course, civilization, from the days in which the Sumerians invented irrigation with canals and artificial rivers to supplement the lack of rainfall (from the Mother's body) on the deserts of the alluvial plain that gave rise to civilization between the Tigris and Euphrates rivers with cultural artifice, has *always* consisted in the construction of technological supplements and substitutes for the mother's body.

The difference nowadays is only a matter of degree.

We no longer *need* the Great Mother, for we can now perform her own uteromorphic feats better without her. In the post-metaphysical age, technology trumps Nature.

(2014)

Notes

Preface

1. For "Visions of a Biomechanical Apocalypse," see *Lapis* #5, 1997, although the essay has been slightly rewritten and polished up for inclusion in the present volume. The Lapis essay was expanded, revised and changed completely to become a chapter in my second book *Celluloid Heroes & Mechanical Dragons*, but it scarcely resembles its original prototype, which is why I have included it here and called the "First Version." For "Ancient Myth and Modern Science," see *Parabola* magazine, Fall, 2008, although here again I have revised and slightly rewritten the essay.

2. See Gianni Vattimo, *A Farewell to Truth*, trans. William McCuaig, (Columbia University Press, 2014).

3. For instance, see William Irwin Thompson, *Imaginary Landscape: Making Worlds of Myth and Science* (NY: Palgrave Macmillan, 1989) or Misia Landau, *Narratives of Human Evolution* (Yale University Press, 1991).

4. See "How the 'True World' Finally Became a Fable" in *Twilight of the Idols*, collected in *The Portable Nietzsche*, ed. and trans. Walter Kaufmann, (NY: Penguin Books, 1968), 485ff.

5. See "The End of Philosophy and the Task of Thinking" in Martin Heidegger, *Basic Writings*, trans. David Farrell Krell (NY: Harper Perennial, 2008), 427ff.

6. Peter Sloterdijk and Hans-Jurgen Heinrichs, *Neither Sun Nor Death*, trans. Steve Corcoran (Los Angeles: Semiotexte, 2011), 167.

7. See the chapter "Mark Rothko" in John David Ebert, *Art After Metaphysics* (NY: Create Space, 2013), 53ff.

8. Martin Heidegger, *Country Path Conversations*, trans. Bret W. Davis (Indiana University Press, 2010), 128.

9. See "Structure, Sign and Play in the Discourse of the Human Sciences," in Jacques Derrida, *Writiing and Difference*, trans. Alan Bass (The University of Chicago Press, 1978), esp. 280.

Visions of a Biomechanical Apocalypse: First Version

10. Oswald Spengler, *Man and Technics* (NY: Alfred A. Knopf, 1932), 103.

11. James Joyce, *Finnegans Wake* (NY: Penguin Classics, 1999), 213.

12. Robinson Jeffers, *The Collected Poetry of Robinson Jeffers: Volume One 1920-1928*, ed. Tim Hunt (Stanford University Press, 1999), 96-97.

13. For my extended reading of Alien, see John David Ebert, *Alien Scene-by-Scene* (NY: Create Space, 2015).

14. For my extended analysis of *Videodrome*, see John David Ebert, *Videodrome Scene-by-Scene* (Eugene, OR: Post Egoism Media, 2016).

15. For Heidegger on the time of the "Between" as he calls it, see Martin Heidegger, *Basic Questions of Philosophy: Selected "Problems" of "Logic,"* trans. Richard Rojcewicz and Andre Schuwer (Indiana University Press, 1994), esp. 131ff.

16. This paragraph is already "pregnant" with my first book, written immediately following this essay. See John David Ebert, *Twilight of the Clockwork God: Conversations on Science and Spirituality at the End of an Age* (San Francisco, CA: Council Oak Books, 1999).

Ancient Myth and Modern Science

17. Joseph Campbell, "The Symbol Without Meaning" in *The Flight of the Wild Gander: Explorations in the Mythological Dimension – Selected Essays, 1944-1968* (Novato, CA: New World Library, 2002), 101.

18. Ibid., 101.

19. Ibid., 98.

20. Ibid., 22.

21. *Upanisads*, trans. Patrick Olivelle (Oxford University Press, 1996), 13-14.

22. J. Nigro Sansonese, *The Body of Myth* (Rochester, Vermont: Inner Traditions / Bear & Co, 1994), 37.

23. Ibid., 36.

24. Jeremy Narby, *The Cosmic Serpent: DNA and the Origins of Knowledge* (NY: Jeremy P. Tarcher / Putnam, 1998).

25. *Upanisads,* trans. Patrick Olivelle, ibid., 127.

26. Mircea Eliade, *Myth and Reality* (NY: Harper and Row, 1963), 22.

27. Robert Graves, *The Greek Myths, Volume One* (NY: George Braziller, Inc., 1959), 30.

28. Paul Davies, *The Fifth Miracle: the Search for the Origin and Meaning of Life* (NY: Simon & Schuster, 1999), 11.

29. Ibid., 26.

30. Ibid., 12.

31. Misia Landau, *Narratives of Human Evolution*

(Yale University Press, 1991).

On the Symbolism of Tools: Hoe and Sickle

32. The Great Stupa at Sanchi in India, for instance, is in the form of an umbrella. See fig. 63 in Heinrich Zimmer, *Myths and Symbols in Indian Art and Civilization*, ed. Joseph Campbell (Princeton University Press, 1972).

33. See, for example, Joseph Campbell, *The Masks of God: Primitive Mythology* (NY: Viking Penguin, 1991), 393.

34. See the link where this myth can be found translated as "The Song of the Hoe" at http://etcsl.orinst.ox.ac.uk/section5/tr554.htm

35. *Myths from Mesopotamia: Creation, the Flood, Gilgamesh and Others*, trans. Stephanie Dalley (Oxford University Press, 1989), 279.

36. See fig. 14 in Joseph Campbell, *The Masks of God: Occidental Mythology* (NY: Viking Penguin, 1991), 49.

37. *The Ancient Egyptian Pyramid Texts*, trans. R.O. Faulkner (Oxford University Press, 1998), 217.

38. Ibid., 211.

39. Ovid, *The Metamorphoses*, trans. Horace Gregory (NY: Viking Press, 1960), 150.

40. *The Homeric Hymns*, trans. Apostolos N. Athanassakis (Baltimore, MD: The Johns Hopkins University Press, 2004), 22-23.

41. Aeschylus, *Prometheus Bound and Other Plays*, trans. Philip Villacott (NY: Penguin Classics, 1961), 31.

42. Robert Graves, *The Greek Myths, Volume One*, ibid., 134.

43. Athanassakis translates it as a "sharp-toothed sickle." See Hesiod, *Theogony, Works and Days, Shield*, trans. Apostolos N. Athanassakis, (Baltimore and London: Johns Hopkins University Press, 1983), 17.

The Farmer Against the Blacksmith: Regarding Some Ancient Sumerian Myths

44. However, the myths associated with Ninurta / Ningirsu as a monster slayer are considerably older than that, since fig. 135 in Jeremy Black and Anthony Green, *Gods, Demons and Symbols of Ancient Mesopotamia: an Illustrated Dictionary*, (Austin, TX: University of Texas Press, 1997) shows Ninurta fighting a seven headed dragon that was found engraved on a shell inlay plaque dating from the Early Dynastic period (c. 3000 BC – 2350 BC).

45. A translation of this text may be found on the Electronic Text Corpus of Sumerian Literature, which can be found online at: http://etcsl.orinst.ox.ac.uk/section1/tr162.htm

46. According to Thorkild Jacobsen, he was known as

"Ningirsu" in the city of Girsu and "Ninurta" in the city of Nippur. See Thorkild Jacobsen, *The Treasures of Darkness: A History of Mesopotamian Religion* (New Haven and London: Yale University Press, 1976), 133.

47. "The plough is captioned as a symbol of Ningirsu on Kassite kudurrus..." See Jeremy Black and Anthony Green, *Gods, Demons and Symbols of Ancient Mesopotamia: an Illustrated Dictionary*, ibid., 142.

48. See Thorkild Jacobsen, *The Treasures of Darkness*, ibid., 127.

49. *The Literature of Ancient Sumer*, trans. Jeremy A. Black, Graham Cunningham, Eleanor Robson and Gabor Zolyomi, (Oxford University Press, 2004), 165.

50. The other eleven are known as the Six-headed Wild Ram, the Seven-headed Snake, the Dragon, the Palm-tree King, the Gypsum, the Strong Copper, the Kuliana, the Magillum-boat, Lord Saman-ana, the Bison-bull and the Imdugud bird. The number 12 is suspicious astronomically, however, and may suggest that these monsters might have been constellations and that Ninurta's deeds are the prototype of the 12 Labors of Hercules. See Jeremy A. Black, *Gods, Demons and Symbols of Ancient Mesopotamia*, ibid., 164.

51. *The Literature of Ancient Sumer*, trans. Jeremy A. Black, ibid., 171-72.

52. Ibid., 176.

53. Jane R. McIntosh, *Ancient Mesopotamia: New Perspectives* (Santa Barbara, CA: ABC Clio, 2005), 244.

54. *The Literature of Ancient Sumer*, ibid., 165.

55. *Gods, Demons and Symbols of Ancient Mesopotamia*, ibid., 36.

56. See Runo 37, "Ilmarinen's Gold and Silver Bride," in *The Kalevala, Epic of the Finnish People*, trans. Eino Friberg (Helsinki, Finlad: Otava Publishing, 1988), 288ff.

57. William Leiss, *The Domination of Nature* (Boston, MA: Beacon Press, 1974), 25-26.

58. *The Literature of Ancient Sumer*, Ibid., 178.

59. See "Ninurta and the turtle: translation" at the Electronic Text Corpus of Sumerian Literature at: http://etcsl.orinst.ox.ac.uk/section1/tr163.htm

60. See the story "Adapa" in Stephanie Dalley, *Myths from Mesopotamia*, ibid., 182.

61. See E.A. Speiser's translation of "Adapa," which includes more of the ending than is translated by Stephanie Dalley. James B. Pritchard, ed. *The Ancient Near East: an Anthology of Texts and Pictures*, (Princeton University Press, 2011), 73ff.

62. George Roux, *Ancient Iraq* (NY: Penguin Books, 1992), 106.

63. Samuel Noah Kramer, *The Sumerians: Their History, Culture and Character* (University of Chicago Press, 1971), 145.

64. Nicholas Campion, *The Great Year: Astrology, Millenarianism and History in the Western Tradition* (NY: Penguin Arkana, 1994), 84-88.

On the Cover Painting: *Prometheus Being Chained by Vulcan*

65. Aeschylus, *Prometheus Bound, The Suppliants, Seven Against Thebes, The Persians*, trans. Philip Vellacott (NY: Penguin Classics, 1961), 20-22.

66. Hesiod, *Theogony, Works and Days, Shield*, trans. Apostolos N. Athanasakkis (Baltimore and London: Johns Hopkins University, 1983), 26-27.

67. Ibid., 26.

68. Aeschylus, *Prometheus Bound*, ibid. 34.

69. Hesiod, *Theogony, Works and Days, Shield*, ibid. 70.

70. See the essays "Building, Dwelling, Thinking" and "The Thing" in Martin Heidegger, *Poetry, Language, Thought*, trans. Albert Hofstadter (NY: Harper Perennial, 2001).

71. Hesiod, *Theogony, Works and Days, Shield*, ibid., 36.

72. See the essay "Our Images" in Vilem Flusser, *Post-History*, trans. Rodrigo Maltez Novaes (Minneapolis, MN: Univocal Publishing, 2013).

73. Marshall McLuhan with Wilford Watson, *From Cliché to Archetype*, ed. W. Terrence Gordon (Berkeley, CA: Gingko Press, 2011), 104.

74. Plato, *The Collected Dialogues, Including the Letters*, eds. Edith Hamilton and Huntington Cairns, (Princeton, NJ: 1989), 821ff.

From the Myth of Tammuz to the Collapse of the Signifieds

75. See Peter Sloterdijk, *Spheres II: Globes, Macrospherology* (Los Angeles: Semiotexte, 2014).

76. See Chapter 9, "The Value Boundary between the Cultural Archive and the Profane Realm" in Boris Groys, *On the New*, trans. G.M. Goshgarian, (London and New York: Verso Books, 2014), 63ff.

77. Edward W. Said, *Orientalism* (NY: Vintage Books, 1979).

78. See the essay, "Structure, Sign and Play in the Discourse of the Human Sciences," in Jacques Derrida, *Writing and Difference*, trans. Alan Bass (The University of Chicago Press, 1978), esp. 280.

79. John David Ebert, *Art After Metaphysics* (NY:

Create Space, 2013), 22-26.

80. Ibid., 59.

81. For Heidegger's essay, "What is Metaphysics?" see Martin Heidegger, *Basic Writings*, ed. David Farrell Krell, (NY: Harper Perennial, 2008), esp. 102ff.

82. See especially Gianni Vattimo, *A Farewell to Truth*, trans. William McCuaig (Columbia University Press, 2014).

83. Gilles Deleuze and Felix Guattari, *Anti-Oedipus, Capitalism and Schizophrenia*, trans. Robert Hurley, Mark Seem and Helen R. Lane (NY: Penguin Classics, 1977).

84. See Chapter 5, "587 BC – AD 70: On Several Regimes of Signs," in Gilles Deleuze and Felix Guattari, *A Thousand Plateaus, Capitalism and Schizophrenia*, trans. Brian Massumi (University of Minnesota Press, 1987), 111ff.

85. Boris Groys, *On the New*, ibid., 65.

86. Edward Gibbon, *The History of the Decline and Fall of the Roman Empire, Volume 1*, ed. David Womersley (NY: Penguin Classics, 1994), 164-166.

87. See "The Caliphate of Baghdad," in Albert Hourani, *A History of the Arab Peoples*, (Cambridge, MA: The Belknap Press of Harvard University Press, 1991), esp. 32-33.

88. For the tale of Ishtar and Tammuz, see *The Ancient Near East: an Anthology of Texts and Pictures*, James B. Pritchard, ed., ibid., 77ff.

89. See "Tablet VIII. The Funeral of Enkidu," in *The Epic of Gilgamesh: A New Translation*, trans. Andrew George, (NY: Barnes and Noble Books, 1999, 62ff.

90. *Eighteen Songs of a Nomad Flute: the Story of Lady Wen-Chi*, trans. Robert A. Rorex, Wen C. Fong (Yale University Press, 2012).

91. See also Jean Gebser's description of this process in "The Three European Worlds," in *The Ever-Present Origin*, trans. Noel Barstad with Algis Mickunas, (Ohio University Press, 1985), esp. 11-15.

92. Robert Payne, *The History of Islam* (New York: Dorset Press, 1959), 130-31.

93. Ibid, 131.

94. This can be tracked by a careful study of Markus Hattstein and Peter Delius, *Islam: Art and Architecture*, (Potsdam, Germany: H.F. Ullman, 2015).

95. John David Ebert, *Art After Metaphysics*, ibid., 22-26.

96. Jacques Derrida, *Writing and Difference*, ibid., 278-80.

Heidegger vs. Coca-Cola

97. Martin Heidegger, *Poetry, Language, Thought,* trans. Albert Hofstadter (NY: Harper Perennial, 1971), 110-111.

98. See the essay "What is Metaphysics?" in Martin Heidegger, *Basic Writings,* ibid., 102ff.

99. Mark Pendergrast, *For God, Country and Coca-Cola: the Definitive History of the Great American Soft Drink and the Company that Makes it* (NY: Basic Books, 203), 25.

100. Ibid., 21.

101. Ibid., 22.

102. Ibid., 6.

103. Ibid., 28.

104. Gyvel Young-Witzel and Michael Karl Witzel, *The Sparkling Story of Coca-Cola: An Entertaining History Including Collectibles, Coke Lore and Calendar Girls* (Stillwater, MN: Voyageur Press, 2002), 17.

105. Pat Watters, *Coca-Cola: an Illustrated History,* (NY: Doubleday, 1978), 16.

106. Ibid., 17.

107. Chris H. Beyer, *Coca-Cola Girls: An Advertis-*

ing Art History (Collectors Press, 2000), 9.

108. Mark Pendergrast, *For God, Country and Coca-Cola*, ibid., 93.

109. Young-Witzel and Michael Karl Witzel, *The Sparkling Story of Coca-Cola*, ibid., 47.

110. Martin Heidegger, *Toward the Definition of Philosophy*, trans. Ted Sadler (London and New York: Continuum Books, 2008), 58-59.

111. Martin Heidegger, *Being and Time*, trans. Joan Macquarrie and Edward Robinson (NY: Harper Perennial, 2008), 147.

112. Martin Heidegger, *Introduction to Phenomenological Research,* trans. Daniel O. Dahlstrom (Indiana University Press, 2005), 139.

113. See the essay "The Question Concerning Technology," in Martin Heidegger, *Basic Writings*, ibid., 321-322.

114. Martin Heidegger, *Being and Time*, ibid., 147.

115. Ibid., 103.

116. Ibid., 102-103.

117. Martin Heidegger, *History of the Concept of Time: Prolegomena*, trans. Theodore Kisiel (Indiana University Press, 1992), 158-163.

118. Young-Witzel and Michael Karl Witzel, *The Sparkling Story of Coca-Cola*, ibid., 48.

119. Ibid., 49.

Ted Kaczynski's Technological Gnosticism

120. Alston Chase, *Harvard and the Unabomber: the Education of an American Terrorist* (New York and London: W.W. Norton & Co., 2003), 49.

121. Ibid., 52.

122. Ibid., 53-54.

123. Ibid., 75.

124. For Nietzsche on Socrates in brief, see the section "The Problem of Socrates" in *Twilight of the Idols* which may be found collected in *The Portable Nietzsche*, ed. Walter Kaufmann (NY: Penguin Books, 1968), 473-479.

125. Theodore Kaczynski, *The Unabomber Manifesto: Industrial Society and its Future* (Madison, Wisconsin: Jolly Roger Press, 1995), 21-22.

126. Ibid., 30.

127. Ibid., 18.

128. Ibid., 56.

129. Ibid., 84-85.

130. For a good synopsis of this cosmology consult "The Apocryphon of John" in *The Nag Hammadi Library*, ed. James M. Robinson (Harper San Francisco, 1988), 104-123.

131. In one of Heidegger's early lectures he calls this *Befindlichkeit*, or disposition. "When we say [Dasein] *finds itself*, this 'itself' first does not really refer expressly to a developed and thematically conscious 'I.' In the very everyday absorption in the Anyone, it can be this Anyone itself in its indeterminacy...This co-discoveredness of being-in-the-world in being solicited by the world is pos-sible only because Dasein originally always *finds itself* in each of its modes of being, because Dasein is discovered for itself. We call this basic form of primary co-discov-eredness of Dasein *disposition.*" See Martin Heidegger, *The History of the Concept of Time: Prolegomena,* ibid., 255.

132. "The first and most vital step of all...is simply to understand media and their revolutionary effects on all psychic and social values and institutions...The central purpose of all my work is to convey this message, that by understanding media as they extend man, we gain a measure of control over them." From "The Playboy Inter-view" collected in *Essential McLuhan*, eds. Eric McLu-han and Frank Zingrone (NY: Basic Books, 1995), 265.

133. Max Horkheimer and Theodor W. Adorno, *Dia-lectic of Enlightenment: Philosophical Fragments*, ed.

Gunzelin Schmid Noerr, trans. Edmund Jephcott (Stanford University Press, 2007), esp. 94ff.

A Few (More) Words on Thomas Pynchon's 1963 Novel *V.*

134. For the concept of "jointure" in the *Contributions*, see *Companion to Heidegger's Contributions to Philosophy*, eds. Charles E. Scott, Susan Schoenbohm, Daniela Vallega-Neu and Alejandro Vallega (Indiana University Press, 2001), 122.

135. For an excellent synopsis of his philosophy of the event, see Alain Badiou, *Ethics: An Essay on the Understanding of Evil*, trans. Peter Hallward (London and New York: Verso Books, 2001).

136. J. Kerry Grant, *A Companion to V.* (Athens and London: University of Georgia Press, 2001), 85.

137. The term "logocentric age" comes from Derrida; see Jacques Derrida, *Of Grammatology*, trans. Gayatry Chakravorty Spivak (Baltimore and London: Johns Hopkins University Press, 1997), 47.

138. See the chapter "The Dynamo and the Virgin" in Henry Adams, *The Education of Henry Adams* (NY: Penguin Classics, 1995), 360ff.

139. Marshall McLuhan, *The Mechanical Bride: Folklore of Industrial Man* (Boston, MA: Beacon Press, 1951).

140. Hans Belting, *Likeness and Presence: A History of the Image Before the Era of Art* (The University of Chicago Press, 1994), esp. 33-34.

141. See the Introduction entitled "On the Four World Ages of Western Art" in John David Ebert, *Art After Metaphysics* (NY: Create Space, 2013) for a more thorough analysis.

142. Eric A. Havelock, *The Muse Learns to Write: Reflections on Orality and Literacy from Antiquity to the Present* (New Haven and London: Yale University Press, 1986).

143. Hans-Georg Gadamer, *Truth and Method* (London and New York: Continuum Books, 2006), 366-367.

144. See the essay "On The Essence of Truth" in Martin Heidegger, *Basic Writings*, ibid., 111ff.

145. Marshall McLuhan, *Understanding Media: the Extensions of Man* (MIT Press, 1994), 260.

146. See the essay "The Codified World" in Vilem Flusser, *Writings*, ed. Andreas Strohl, trans. Erik Eisel (University of Minnesota Press, 2002), 35ff.

147. See Marc-Alain Ouaknin, *The Mysteries of the Alphabet* (Abbeville Press, 1999) for the chapter on the Hebrew letter *vav*.

148. See the opening chapter "Introduction to the Metaphysical Vulva" in John David Ebert, *Alien Scene-*

by-Scene (NY: Create Space, 2015) for more on the paternal womb.

Bibliography

Adams, Henry. *The Education of Henry Adams*. New York: Penguin Classics, 1995.

Aeschylus, *Prometheus Bound and Other Plays*, trans. Philip Vellacott. New York: Penguin Classics, 1961.

The Ancient Egyptian Pyramid Texts, trans. R.O. Faulkner. Oxford University Press, 1998.

The Ancient Near East: an Anthology of Texts and Pictures, ed. James B. Pritchard, Princeton University Press, 2011.

Badiou, Alain. *Ethics: An Essay on the Understanding of Evil*, trans. Peter Hallward. London and New York: Verso Books, 2001.

Belting, Hans. *Likeness and Presence: A History of the Image Before the Era of Art*. University of Chicago Press, 1994.

Beyer, Chris H. *Coca-Cola Girls: An Advertising Art History*. Collectors Press, 2000.

Black, Jeremy. *The Literature of Ancient Sumer*, trans. Jeremy Black, Graham Cunningham, Eleanor Robson and Gabor Zolyomi. Oxford University Press, 2004.

___. and Green, Anthony. *Gods, Demons and Symbols of Ancient Mesopotamia: an Illustrated Dictionary*. Austin, TX: University of Texas Press, 1997.

Campbell, Joseph. *The Flight of the Wild Gander: Explorations in the Mythological*

Dimension—Selected Essays, 1944-1968. New World Library, 2002.

___. The Masks of God: Primitive Mythology. New York: Viking Penguin, 1991.

Campion, Nicholas. The Great Year: Astrology, Millenarianism and History in the Western Tradition. New York: Penguin Arkana, 1994.

Chase, Alston. Harvard and the Unabomber: the Education of an American Terrorist. New York and London: W.W. Norton & Co., 2003.

Companion to Heidegger's Contributions to Philosophy, eds. Charles E. Scott, Susan Schoenbohm, Daniela Vallega-Neu and Alejandro Vallega. Indiana University Press, 2001.

Dalley, Stephanie. Myths from Mesopotamia: Creation, the Flood, Gilgamesh and Others, ed. and trans. Stephanie Dalley. Oxford University Press, 1989.

Davies, Paul. The Fifth Miracle: the Search for the Origin and Meaning of Life. New York: Simon & Schuster, 1999.

Deleuze, Gilles and Guattari, Felix. Anti-Oedipus, Capitalism and Schizophrenia, trans. Robert Hurley, Mark Seem and Helen R. Lane. New York: Penguin Classics, 1977.

___. and ___. A Thousand Plateaus, Capitalism and Schizophrenia, trans. Brian Massumi. University of Minnesota Press, 1987.

Derrida, Jacques. Writing and Difference, trans. Alan Bass. The University of Chicago Press, 1978.

___. Of Grammatology, trans. Gayatry Chakravorty Spivak. Baltimore and London: Johns Hopkins University Press, 1997.

Ebert, John David. Alien Scene-by-Scene. New York: Create Space, 2015.

___. Art After Metaphysics. New York: Create Space, 2013.

____. *Celluloid Heroes & Mechanical Dragons: Film as the Mythology of the Electronic Age*. Christchurch, New Zealand: Cybereditions, 2005.

____. *Twilight of the Clockwork God: Conversations on Science and Spirituality at the End of an Age*. San Francisco, CA: Council Oak Books, 1999.

____. *Videodrome Scene-by-Scene*. Eugene, OR: Post Egoism Media, 2016.

Eighteen Songs of a Nomad Flute: the Story of Lady Wen-Chi, trans. Robert A. Rorex, Wen C. Fong. Yale University Press, 2012.

Eliade, Mircea. *Myth and Reality*. New York: Harper and Row, 1963.

Flusser, Vilem. *Post-History*, trans. Rodrigo Novaes. Minneapolis, MN: Univocal Publishing, 2013.

____. *Writings*, ed. Andreas Strohl, trans. Erik Eisel. University of Minnesota Press, 2002.

Gadamer, Hans-Georg. *Truth and Method*. London and New York: Continuum Books, 2006.

Gebser, Jean. *The Ever-Present Origin*, trans. Noel Barstard with Algis Mickunas. Ohio University Press, 1985.

George, Andrew. *The Epic of Gilgamesh: A New Translation*, ed. and trans. Andrew George. New York: Barnes and Noble Books, 1999.

Gibbon, Edward. *The History of the Decline and Fall of the Roman Empire, Volume 1*, ed. David Womersley. New York: Penguin Classics, 1994.

Grant, J. Kerry. *A Companion to V.* Athens and London: University of Georgia Press, 2001.

Graves, Robert. *The Greek Myths: Volume One*. New York: George Braziller, Inc., 1959.

Groys, Boris. *On the New*, trans. G.M. Goshgarian. London and New York: Verso Books, 2014.

Hattstein, Markus and Delius, Peter. *Islam: Art and Architecture.* Potsdam, Germany: H.F. Ullman, 2015.

Havelock, Eric A. *The Muse Learns to Write: Reflections of Orality and Literacy from Antiquity to the Present.* New Haven and London: Yale University Press, 1986.

Heidegger, Martin. *Basic Questions of Philosophy: Selected "Problems" of "Logic,"* trans. Richard Rojcewicz and Andre Schuwer. Indiana University Press, 1994.

____. *Basic Writings,* trans. David Farrell Krell. New York: Harper Perennial, 2008.

____. *Being and Time,* trans. Joan Macquarrie and Edward Robinson. New York: Harper Perennial, 2008.

____. *Country Path Conversations,* trans. Bret W. Davis. Indiana University Press, 2010.

____. *History of the Concept of Time: Prolegomena,* trans. Theodore Kisiel. Indiana University Press, 1992.

____. *Introduction to Phenomenological Research,* trans. Daniel O. Dahlstrom. Indiana University Press, 2005.

____. *Poetry, Language, Thought,* trans. Albert Hofstadter. New York: Harper Perennial, 2001.

____. *Toward the Definition of Philosophy,* trans. Ted Sadler. London and New York: Continuum Books, 2008.

Hesiod, *Theogony, Works and Days, Shield,* trans. Apostolos N. Athanassakis. Baltimore and London: The Johns Hopkins University Press, 1983.

The Homeric Hymns, trans. Apostolos N. Athanassakis. Baltimore, MD: The Johns Hopkins University Press, 2004.

Horkheimer, Max and Adorno, Theodor W. *Dialectic of Englightenment: Philosophical Fragments,* ed. Gunzelin Schmid Noerr, trans. Edmund Jephcott. Stanford University Press, 2007.

Hourani, Albert. *A History of the Arab Peoples.* Cambridge, MA: The Belknap Press of Harvard University Press,

1991.

Jacobsen, Thorkild. *The Treasures of Darkness: a History of Mesopotamian Religion*. New Haven and London: Yale University Press, 1976.

Jeffers, Robinson. *The Collected Poetry of Robinson Jeffers: Volume One, 1920-1928*, ed. Tim Hunt. Stanford University Press, 1999.

Joyce, James. *Finnegans Wake*. New York: Penguin Classics, 1999.

Kaczynski, Theodore. *The Unabomber Manifesto: Industrial Society and its Future*. Madison, Wisconsin: Jolly Roger Press, 1995.

The Kalevala, Epic of the Finnish People, trans. Eino Friberg. Helsinki, Finland: Otava Publishing, 1988.

Kramer, Samuel Noah. *The Sumerians: Their History, Culture and Character*. University of Chicago Press, 1971.

Landau, Misia. *Narratives of Human Evolution*. Yale University Press, 1991.

Leiss, William. *The Domination of Nature*. Boston, MA: Beacon Press, 1974.

McIntosh, Jane R. *Ancient Mesopotamia: New Perspectives*. Santa Barbara, CA: ABC Clio, 2005.

McLuhan, Marshall. *Essential McLuhan*, eds. Eric McLuhan and Frank Zingrone. New York: Basic Books, 1995.

___. *The Mechanical Bride: Folklore of Industrial Man*. Boston, MA: Beacon Press, 1951.

___. *Understanding Media: the Extensions of Man*. MIT Press, 1994.

___. with Wilford Watson, *From Cliché to Archetype*, ed. W. Terence Gordon. Berkeley, CA: Gingko Press, 2011.

Narby, Jeremy. *The Cosmic Serpent: DNA and the Origins of Knowledge*. New York: Jeremy P. Tarcher / Putnam,

1998.

Nietzsche, Friedrich. *The Portable Nietzsche*, trans. Walter Kaufmann. New York: Penguin Books, 1968.

Ovid, *The Metamorphoses*, trans. Horace Gregory. New York: Viking Press, 1960

Ouaknin, Marc-Alain. *The Mysteries of the Alphabet.* Abbeville Press, 1999.

Payne, Robert. *The History of Islam.* New York: Dorset Press, 1959.

Pendergrast, Mark. For God, *Country and Coca-Cola: the Definitive History of the Great American Soft Drink and the Company that Makes it.* New York: Basic Books, 2013.

Plato, *The Collected Dialogues, Including the Letters*, ed. Edith Hamilton and Huntington Cairns. Princeton, N.J.: 1989.

Robinson, James M. *The Nag Hammadi Library.* Harper Sa Francisco, 1988.

Roux, George. *Ancient Iraq.* New York: Penguin Books, 1992.

Said, Edward W. *Orientalism.* New York: Vintage Books, 1979.

Sansonese, J. Nigro. *The Body of Myth.* Rochester, VT: Inner Traditions / Bear & Co. 1994.

Sloterdijk, Peter. *Spheres II: Globes, Macrospherology.* Los Angeles: Semiotexte, 2014.

___. and Heinrichs, Hans-Jurgen. *Neither Sun Nor Death*, trans. Steve Corcoran. Los Angeles: Semiotexte, 2011.

Spengler, Oswald. *Man and Technics*, trans. Charles Francis Atkinson. New York: Alfred A. Knopf, 1932.

Thompson, William Irwin. *Imaginary Landscape: Making Worlds of Myth & Science.* New York: Palgrave Macmillan, 1989.

Upanishads, trans. Patrick Olivelle. Oxford University Press, 1996.

Vattimo, Gianni. *A Farewell to Truth*, trans. William McCuaig. Columbia University Press, 2014.

Watters, Pat. *Coca-Cola: an Ilustrated History*. New York: Doubleday, 1978.

Young-Witzel, Gyvel and Witzel, Michael Karl. *The Sparkling Story of Coca-Cola: An Entertaining History Including Collectibles, Coke Lore and Calendar Girls*. Stillwater, MN: Voyageur Press, 2002.

Zimmer, Heinrich. *Myths and Symbols in Indian Art and Civilization*, ed. Joseph Campbell. Princeton University Press, 1972.

Made in the USA
Las Vegas, NV
07 November 2022

58996003R00111